SURVIVING

the

15-Second

Resume Read

SURVIVING

the
15-Second
Resume Read

Peggy O. Swager

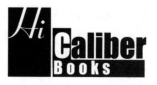

Acknowledgements:
Cover Design: Linda Bollinger, britemeado@aol.com
Initial content and copy editing: Bonnie Granat, www.editors-writers.info
Final content and copy editing: Roger Christiansen, aa0vo@juno.com

ISBN 0-9726526-0-4

Library of Congress Cataloging: Pending — please visit web site at www.hi-caliberbooks.com

Attention Corporations, Recruiters, Job Agencies, Universities, Colleges, Professional Organizations, and Teachers: Quantity discounts are available on bulk purchases of this book. Please contact Hi-Caliber Books at P.O. Box 807, Monument, CO 80132, phone 719-481-0056, www.hi-caliberbooks.com.

Contents

Chapter 1

A Behind the Scenes Look at the Employment Business

> Few people understand the entire process of hiring an employee. Job recruiters are in a unique position to understand this process, because they deal with both job candidates and employers.

The Role of Recruiters

Companies that have a position that requires a top performer rather than an average performer sometimes turn to recruiters to find that key individual. In exchange for a fee, the recruiter finds a few top candidates for their clients to choose from and then guarantees that the employee selected will stay at a position for a certain length of time. Recruiters are heavily invested in finding the right person for the position they are filling. In addition to their guarantee, the recruiters know that good placements lead to more contracts with a company and a good reputation throughout the industry. Recruiters use resumes to present their candidates to a client. The resume is carefully tooled to deliver information to the client and presents exactly the skills a candidate has that relate to performing the job.

How Recruiters do Their Jobs

Job Analysis

Recruiters attack a job placement from several angles. First they develop a clear understanding of what the client's needs are for the position. Part of a recruiter's job analysis includes listing each functional area for which the job is accountable, listing the key results anticipated in each of the functional areas, and analyzing the key problems the client hopes to solve by filling this position. Recruiters then determine what knowledge and skills a candidate must possess. A job analysis is more than just a job description. Recruiters want to know the history of the position, the advancement opportunities, the expectations of the client, the compensation, and the culture of the company.

Culture is Important

The recruiter assesses the employer's work culture, which includes the character, style, personality, and philosophy of the company. Some companies that have favored technical fit over cultural fit find they lose an employee they worked hard to acquire. This kind of loss costs both the employer and the employee dearly. For a recruiter, it means starting a search over with no additional compensation.

The fit of an employee to the working culture makes a great difference in the length of time and overall productivity of that employee. For example, some people thrive in a relaxed, blue-jean environment, while others may prefer more professional attire and behavior around the office. For some, a carefully structured hierarchy is ideal. For others, a friendly interchange of ideas and a boss they can easily approach works best. Some people thrive in a chaotic atmosphere that is fast-paced, viewing anything less dynamic as boring. Others become unraveled in this type of environment and won't be able to function at all. There is no right or wrong assessment for a company—the only *wrong* is when a person is mismatched to a work culture.

The Hiring Process

After a company and recruiter sign a contract, the recruiter spends time on the phone with the company to determine the company's needs. The recruiter develops a clear description of the job and the goals of the company in filling the position. The recruiter investigates the current issues at the company, and the specific current need that the individual hired for this position is going to satisfy. Next, the recruiter analyzes the company's culture—its character, style, personality, and philosophy. The recruiter asks how the company's culture compares to similar companies in the industry. The questions asked include how the company handles conflict and whether the company is happy with its current culture. Finally, the recruiter asks how the company will assess a new employee's success in the position, and what the advancement opportunities and expectations are for that employee.

The recruiter starts to work by searching the recruiting database, where candidates are listed by education, job title, job skills, and years of experience. Most recruiting agencies maintain their own databases. There are several ways that information about job candidates may enter a recruiting database: the recruiter networked with the individual, a recruiter found a suitable resume on the Internet, or an individual randomly sent in a resume.

Recruiting agencies receive unsolicited resumes all the time. Resumes that clearly show job skills and work history that recruiters can use are entered into the database. Poor quality resumes are thrown in the trash. The only time a recruiter accepts a poor resume is when the recruiter has solicited a resume from an individual. Typically, this individual was first contacted by phone. A short interview was conducted to determine abilities. If the recruiter feels a candidate is a good fit for the job, the recruiter asks for references. If those references check out, the recruiter will ask for a recent resume. In such a case, if the resume is of poor quality, the recruiter will rework it until it is a high-quality resume and suitable to send to the company.

When first working to fill a job position, recruiters turn to their database. If there are no qualified candidates in a recruiter's database, the recruiter picks up the telephone. Calls are made to people they know who work in a similar industry for which the recruiter is searching for a candidate. If that fails, the recruiter engages in headhunting by contacting different companies and finding out who is holding a similar position. When the recruiter finds the name of a person in the same job they are trying to fill, they contact that person and start the process of seducing them away from their current job.

After a few good candidates are located and screened, the recruiter sends the candidate's resumes to the client. The recruiter makes sure each resume appropriately highlights information about the candidate that the company needs to know. During the review process, a client often sends the resume via fax machine or email to other individuals in their company who are involved in the decision process. After a resume is reviewed, the recruiting agency is contacted about which candidates will receive an interview. Once the company interviews and chooses to make an offer to one candidate, the recruiter assists the company in its contract negotiations.

Advantages of Using Recruiters

For both employer and employee/candidate, there are obvious advantages to using a recruiter. The employer has a skilled person who will weed through the thousands of candidates available for the position. The employee/candidate has someone who seeks out top performers. If someone the recruiter respects recommends an employee/candidate, the recruiter will accept a low-quality resume. The recruiter will turn that poor resume into a competent one.

The Disadvantage of Using Recruiters

The disadvantage exists only for companies. Recruiters cost companies money. For many positions, it isn't practical to use them. A recruiter won't take on some positions because a recruiter usually charges a percentage of the first year's salary, and low annual income don't pay enough to become involved.

Interviews with the Professionals

A Look at the Business of Placing Employees

Mike Guberman has over thirty years of experience in recruiting and owns The Guberman Company, an executive recruiting agency. When asked about the industry and recruiting in general, Mike said:

> Cycles can change every six months; however, top-notch, high-performance people are always in demand. The characteristics of top performers include their ability to add value to the company that wants them.

For Mike, some cycles make these key people more difficult to obtain. When the needs in industry are greater, Mike says that top performers drive costs up.

Mike explains that for a while the industry went through a trend where changing jobs was okay. It was the acceptable standard for candidates to change jobs without hurting their future employment prospects. This is no longer true. Both companies and recruiters now look unfavorably at people who change jobs often, except of course in the high-tech industry.

When asked how things have changed over the years, Mike said:

> Today's employer is focused more than ever before on an individual's ability to fit into the culture of the company. At one time, companies only sought to hire

the top performers; now companies realize that who they hire must also fit into their organization. This is an issue that needs great attention not only by the employer, but by the potential employee. Companies are now more able than ever before to identify their cultures, which allows them to identify who will fit into their environment. A lot is involved in evaluating the culture of a company, and employers now have the ever-increasing burden of seeing where company is going and how a potential candidate is going to fit into that vision of the future.

Mike explains that candidates need to play an active role in securing their future at a company. According to Mike:

> Candidates can help themselves by learning how to focus on their ability to fit into a company, even if the company doesn't pursue the culture issue. An employee needs to understand what his own value system is all about and the kind of culture where he performs best. For instance, a person needs to know if he or she works best as a loner, or if he or she excels in a fast track and moving environment. Some people do their best in highly structured cultures whereas others need room to pursue their creativity. The bottom line is that you need to explore who you are and where you will fit. What maybe a great culture for one person may not fit you at all.

What Recruiters Say About Resumes

Howard Epstein worked with placing people in the printing and graphic arts industries. For over 12 years, he placed people in manufacturing positions in those industries from line supervisors to vice presidents. He holds a masters in psychology and uses his degree when dealing with the human factor of his job to assess people's strengths and employers' needs. A lot of resumes crossed his desk over the years. Some he'd asked for, and others came in on speculation.

Howard worked as both a resume reader and a resume writer. As a reader, he viewed resumes from the perspective of a company that needs to assess a person's potential for a position. As a resume writer, he helped tailor information from his candidates before presenting the resume to a client. Here are some of the things Howard says about reading a resume:

> For me, resumes I've asked to see get a lot more consideration than those that are sent in on speculation. Often I will get a recommendation about a candidate from someone I respect in the field. I'll call that person and do a phone interview. If things progress positively, I'll ask to see a resume. When I get that resume, I like to read the resume backwards, starting on page two. Specific skills are necessary for some resumes, but only work as filler for more senior people. I want to see what that person was responsible for and what he or she accomplished in a job.

> On that second page, I look to see where this person started out in life, beginning with their education. This gives me a flow that shows how a person has progressed in their professional career. As a business recruiter, I need to get

a feel for the person so I can sense if they will fit with the culture of the business where I'm working to make a placement.

Resumes that come to me on speculation, where someone just sends it to me uninvited, are another case. What people say about only giving a resume a fifteen-second reading is true. In those seconds of reading, I want to know if what the person has done is applicable to my needs for filling a job now or in the future. I want a resume that looks like what I'm used to looking at; one that is well organized. At a glance, I want to know where the person worked, what they did, and how long they did it. I don't have a lot of time to dig out what I need to know.

There are certain problems on a resume that get it immediately thrown out. One thing is if the type is too small. I already know this person has tried to squeeze down print instead of editing the resume. If they don't have the time to edit, I don't have the time to read. Other things that are the kiss of death include: typos, grammatical errors, and misspelled words. Also, the resume needs to be on plain white paper.

In general, Howard states that a good resume should be written to fit the person and the position. It is okay for someone who is applying for a position as a graphic designer or someone in the entertainment field to have a more artsy resume, but that won't work for other industries. With most jobs, the resume recipients are more conservative and traditional. For those jobs, you need a conventional resume.

A good resume needs to succinctly tell the story of who this person is, their experience, their past performance, and accomplishments. The resume needs to reveal to the reader the person's position, achievements, and responsibilities and it must do so in a way that requires little effort on the part of the reader. People need to understand the career field they are competing in and only include in their resume things that relay the important information about the position for which they are applying. Howard doesn't care to see information about insignificant jobs, and he doesn't care if the first job was at Safeway as a bag boy.

Howard recommends that people do some homework and find out about the company and field they work in. He suggests using the Internet for information and joining professional organizations related to the field. Professional organizations provide valuable networking opportunities.

Other Guidelines Howard Has for a Resume

A resume shouldn't be more than two pages for regular positions. Some people will only have one page. More than two pages means a person hasn't done their work of editing down the information.

Be honest in what you write. People will eventually find out the truth and lying will kill your career. If you tell the truth, you only have to remember one story.

Don't let someone else write your resume. You need to have the resume reflect who you are and what you are all about. Howard has talked to people who didn't know what was on their resume. Immediately, he says good-bye and concludes that these people were either lying, or stupid, or someone else did their resume and they didn't take the time to read it. If they don't take the time, he won't either.

Lastly, Howard says to remember that jobs are subject to the "law of supply and demand." You need a great resume in most career fields. It is a giant business card that you give out to get you an interview, not to get you hired. Use it as an introduction.

Jim Traynor has worked as a recruiter specializing in sales personnel for more than 12 years. Jim says, "The purpose of a resume is to get a company to talk to you. You need to have the resume reader wanting to hear more." Here are some of the things Jim says about a resume:

> When you prepare the sales resume, you need to elaborate on what is sold, how much is sold, and where the product is sold. Just to say you sold brochures for a company isn't enough. You need to state if you sold those brochures as direct mail, and if they were personalized. Tell the resume reader if those brochures were sent to the public (newsstand/mailed) or to companies. Another example is when a sales representative only states they sell hardware computers, they leave the client guessing what kind of hardware. Even worse is a resume that states the sales representative worked in the computer industry. Now the employer has a multitude of generalizations that may not match that employer's needs.

> When reporting how much you sold, state more than numbers. A sales representative may say they sold $1.5M, but that isn't enough information. The employer needs to know if that $1.5 million was in gross or valuated sales. Valuated sales, also called value-added sales, represent the net amount of revenue. For instance if the sales representative sold $5M gross, after subtracting $2.70M for paper, ink and the print run, the valuated sale was $2.30M.

> Potential employers want to know your physical location, where the clients are that you sold to, and what kind of clients you call on. That way, if a sales representative has a lot of connections in the New York market, and the employer needs those kinds of contacts, he or she knows this person will make a good fit.

In place of an overview, Jim uses notes at the end of the resume to highlight the candidate's potential and skills. This is the area where Jim leaves the company with a hunger to learn more by talking with the candidate. Just like the overview, the notes summarize what characteristics the candidate has that would interest that particular company. The notes include information like the following:

> During tenure at Brochure World, starting off with no house accounts, built a brochure sales business to $3M in gross annual sales in two years. Modified the company's marketing plans to include personal follow-ups with key customers.

The notes section describes how a person became successful in a job, but the information must be kept as a brief summary. It is fine to leave the employer with the feeling of needing to know a little more information. That "little more" is the information that belongs in an interview. The resume has served its purpose by giving the employer just enough information to know that this is a viable candidate. The work history describes what was sold and where, and the summary briefly describes how the items were sold. If the needs of the employer and the talents of the candidate match so far, the candidate will get an interview. If things don't match, the client and candidate will not waste each other's time.

Front-Line Resume Readers Tell How They Sort Through Resumes

Michelle McShane works at a recruiting firm as one of the key people who find good candidates. While the recruiters work with the companies to help define just what kind of person they need for a position, Michelle McShane works to help find that person. Her job involves wading through resumes and doing Internet searches for qualified people. When she is evaluating information, she has specifics in mind, including what she is looking for in an ideal employee, exactly what the company is looking for, and what is important to the position she is working to fill. To become more efficient, she has devised techniques for reviewing resumes.

For Michelle, the most important information is the candidate's company experience (work history) and what they accomplished at their previous jobs. When asked how long it takes her to review a resume, she says that if she finds something immediately interesting, she will then read every line on a resume. Often what interests her is work experience that is similar to that required by the job she is trying to fill.

Things that flunk out a resume for Michelle are: misspellings and grammar errors. She also doesn't like a resume that starts out, "When I was here, I did..." She just wants the facts such as: Sold $4M in the first year and went on to...

Sometimes Michelle finds a candidate who has a work history at a company where she is interested in recruiting, but who doesn't have impressive accomplishments for that position. Although many employers will pass such a person by, Michelle will sometimes call the person up for a more detailed interview. If what she learns during the interview shows promise, she will work with the person to help refine the resume so that it includes information about what that person accomplished.

Things Michelle hates to see on resumes include bad fonts, strange indents, and strange, out-of-the-ordinary things. She just wants a resume that is easy to read, simple, and to the point.

When Michelle sees vague statements like reduced costs 15% by eliminating waste; she will challenge these numbers. She needs to know how this was accomplished.

Things she never looks at include the personal interest section, the statement that offers references, and information about hobbies or social groups.

Things she wants to see include education and relevant educational achievements, successful work histories at relevant companies, and work dates that make sense.

Some of the questions she is likely to ask include the following for people who have worked at the same place a long time: What type of challenges did they have in their jobs? What kind of special projects did they work on? Are they willing to learn something new? Are they at all concerned about making a move and not fitting into another culture?

Jody Richardson works at an executive recruiting firm that handles a wide variety of job placements. Her company may look at an average of 250 resumes in one day, and she also searches the Internet and accepts emails. When the company reviews a resume for consideration, it uses several criteria for accepting and rejecting a candidate.

Jody's company knows the client for whom they are doing the search, and sometimes looks for little things on a resume that help in the selection of a potential candidate. These "little things" are hard to summarize. For Jody's company, what makes a difference in a submitted resume is job history. If the resume has no job history, her company has no interest. Her company shies away from people who have poor work histories, such as four jobs in the last three years. Her company understands that sometimes things happen that causes people to have such a work history, but the history needs a good explanation. If the person has been doing contract or consulting work, a less solid job history is fine. When reviewing a job history, Jody looks at how long a person worked at each company, and if the person received promotions at a company where the person worked for an extended period of time.

Another factor Jody considers is the applicant's education. Some of Jody's clients have certain educational requirements for a job. Other information like willingness to relocate and salary requirements she feels belong in a cover letter.

If an applicant is looking for a job in another field, Jody wants to be told upfront about the applicant's intentions and what the applicants capabilities are that relate to a different career. Certain jobs can cross over, for example good sales people can sell almost any product, however, some companies are not willing to allow the time for the newcomer to get up to speed on a product (the learning curve) because for some products, the learning curve is quite steep.

A Seasoned Staffing Recruiter's Point of View

Rick Brown works at a staffing agency and handles technical placements such as technical writers, engineers, programmers, PC technicians, and graphic designers. His company supplies temporary employees or temp-to-perm placements. A large part of his job entails combing over resumes.

When asked how long Rick spends on an initial reading of a resume, he quickly answers, "fifteen seconds." Rick looks to see if the candidate has the primary skills he needs. If those skills are there, he will look further at the resume. According to Rick, fifteen seconds is all the time a lot of employers put into their initial review. Therefore, the skills information must be broken out into its own column so the people reading the resume can find it quickly.

When asked what he likes and doesn't like to see on a resume, Rick quickly replies, "Work dates, the resume needs to have work dates." Rick explains that some people want to submit a functional resume, but that does him no good. He wants to see a summary at the beginning (the part this book calls an overview) followed by a work history. Key words (terms that identify skills in that particular profession and are readily recognized by employers) and a good skills section are also both important. Rick does not want to see any personal information like age or gender. An employer cannot by law ask personal information, so if it is on a resume, Rick has it immediately removed. Other items to leave off a resume are pictures and graphics. A lot of the resumes Rick sees are either faxed or scanned in so they can be sent to companies by email. Pictures and graphics don't transfer in those mediums. Also, pictures and graphics do nothing to sell the person, but instead are as unwelcome as other personal information. Rick says that when you're working on your resume, keep in mind that a resume's function is not to get you a job, but to get you an interview. Your skills, personality, and abilities secure the job.

Rick's preferred order of elements in a resume include:

- Name, address, and other contact information
- Overview
- Professional work experience
- Education
- Training and other information categories

Chapter 2

How Employers Do a Fifteen-Second Read
As Compared to a More Thorough Resume Review

> **What are the most common mistakes people make when creating their resumes?**
> They think of themselves and not the employer to whom they are sending the resume.
>
> **What is a common misconception when people submit their resumes?**
> People think that because they wrote it down it will be read, even if they had to use a small font size to squeeze it into two pages.

Why the Industry Has Gone to a Fifteen-Second Read

Put yourself in the shoes of an employer. Let's say you have a job you need to fill. You place an ad and within a few days you have received 100 resumes in response to that ad. (In tough job markets, this number may be much larger.) If you take five minutes to read each resume (poorly written ones will take longer), you will spend almost eight and a half hours reviewing resumes. Even if you have the time, will you have the endurance to give your full attention to that much material for that long?

Let's say you decide to do a fifteen-second initial read instead. Using that kind of review allows you to easily select your more viable candidates in less than one hour.

If you reduce the initial stack with the fifteen-second read, you can now more thoroughly review your more viable candidates. Because resumes that can withstand a fifteen-second read are typically well-written, you can review the remaining resumes to select five or ten good candidates to interview.

Example of a Fifteen-Second Read

Let's say that Steve Anderson has applied to your company for a position as Vice President of Sales. You pick up his resume (page 12) and in fifteen seconds here is what you can determine.

- At Images.com he was Vice President of Sales for the last few years. On page two, you see he worked for Odellee for nine years (a respectable amount of time).

- At Odellee, he started as a Sales Executive, became a Regional Sales Manager, and quit after becoming Vice President of Sales.
- You glance at his education and see he has a master's in sales and marketing and a bachelor's in human resource management.

You are tempted to review the resume further, but the other ninety-nine resumes are waiting. You put Steve's resume in a pile to review in more depth at a later time.

Steve Anderson's More Thorough Resume Review

The approach to a more thorough resume read is typically different from the fifteen-second read. Here are some of the things you can learn from a more in-depth reading of a well-written resume.

First, you are pleased that it is easy to find this candidate's name on the resume. You glance at his address and note that it is easy to locate and read. You've had resumes in the past that had such small print for the name and address that you almost could not read the information. Then, when you faxed that resume to the home office for review, you got a call because no one could read the resume. Your work was interrupted while you found the resume and read the information over the phone.

Next, you look at the overview. Steve's overview has key items that summarize and point out the things that impressed you about him as an applicant when you conducted your fifteen-second read. You notice he states that he has ten years of sales experience in the printing industry. You quickly look over the job history for evidence of this. The boldface dates are easy to find and it is easy to verify Steve's statement. You put a star on the front page next to "over ten years of sales experience in the printing industry."

Next, you see that Steve has Fortune 500 experience. This is a plus. So is the human resources talent. You take a moment to see where there is evidence of his human resource talent. You find it under education. Steve has a BS in Human Resource Management. Where else? You don't take time to look, but decide to ask during the interview. You make a note on his resume next to his education information.

Next, you look closely at the job history. You notice that Steve has only worked at Images.com for a couple of years as VP of Sales. You turn to the next page and clearly see Steve has a solid nine-year history at Odelle, one of your respected competitors. Below the company name you see asterisks next to the various positions he held at Odelle. At a glance, you know that he worked as a sales executive for six years, as a regional sales manager for two years, and as a vice president of sales and marketing for one year. You make a note to ask him why he left Odelle.

The information in the bulleted area is also easy to read and understand. You take a moment and skim through the bullets about Steve's experience at Odelle for successes similar to those stated for Images.com. On the first page next to his name, you jot down a notation that he is a strong candidate.

STEVE ANDERSON

**1019 Laura Lane
San Jose, California 95125
Home: 408-225-2625
Mobile: 605-678-4251
Kevin@aol.com**

OVERVIEW:

- Over ten years of sales experience in the printing industry.
- Proven leader and manager with a wide array of successes from product groups inside Fortune 500 organizations to successful new product/business launches.
- Experienced recruiter, trainer, and leader of human resources talent.
- Highly Internet and software-fluent.
- Motivated to not only succeed, but do the best.

PROFESSIONAL EXPERIENCE:

Images.com — Palo Alto, CA   *1999–Present*

* *Vice President of Sales*

Images.com was the first on-line printing broker. Joined the company as employee #47; the company has grown to 250 people. Currently in charge of sales and sales development in the United States.

- Recruited sales representatives, and then built field operations from four people and two offices to 78 people and 20 offices.
- Headed "live product" launch in October 1999. Grew contracts from zero to over 343 by July 2000.
- Personally led sales effort to win ten Fortune 500 companies, including General Electric, Ameritech, and Bank of America.
- Grew sales from $100K in 1999 to over $10M in 2000.
- Developed sales metrics, sales model, sales forecast, product marketing plans, and technical certification programs.
- Initiated marketing and business development to drive leveraged sales channels and partnership network, value proposition, pricing models, and vertical market branding.

Odellee & Sons, New York, NY   *1990–1999*

* *Vice President for Sales and Marketing, Prepress Division (1998–1999)*

- Chosen to run national sales and marketing efforts for this new high-growth division.
- Responsible for four major product groups.
- Grew business 200% in one year.
- Directly responsible for twelve sales executives and product managers.
- Developed entire revenue budget using product group, commission plans, metrics, and forecasting tools.

* *Regional Sales Manager, Northwest Division (1996–1998)*

- Managed seven sales executives in nine regions which grossed over $1 billion in gross sales.
- Grew region from $80M to $145M in two years.
- Achieved highest percentage top-line and bottom-line growth rate for both years in entire corporate sales.
- Heavily involved in corporate-wide strategic planning process as well as major capital appropriation projects during both years.

* *Sales Executive (1990–1996)*

- Top producing sales executive in the history of the company.
- Generated over $200M in annual sales.
- Awarded "Sales Rookie of the Year" in 1991.
- Awarded "Sales Representative of the Year" four years in a row.

EDUCATION:

MS, Sales and Marketing, Temple University, Philadelphia, PA, 1989
BS, Human Resource Management, Temple University, Philadelphia, PA, 1986

Some Resumes Don't Even Receive a Full Fifteen-Second Read

Take a look at the Joseph D. Fisk resume on page (16). This is a well-organized and professional resume and the style is appealing. Because it is a resume for a technical field, resume readers will determine in *less* than fifteen seconds if they will review the resume in more detail. They will do this by turning to the second page and looking for key skills. In that initial resume review, no other qualities matter. If those skills are clearly shown, the resume will be reviewed in more detail. If those skills aren't present, the resume will be rejected. On some resumes, the skills are present, but they are not found at a glance. Such resumes are often rejected because it takes too much time to determine if the candidate is qualified.

Roland Stewart's Fifteen Second Read (page 18)

More and more fields of employment that didn't previously require a resume now use resumes as the first line of contact between company and candidate. Although smaller businesses typically receive fewer resumes and sometimes take more time to read a resume, a well-organized resume sells a person's ability to do the job to companies of all sizes.

When Roland Stewart (Butch) called to inquire about applying for a job at Landford Construction Company, the owner of the company told him to come in at seven a.m. The owner said he only had a short amount of time to see Butch, but he added that if Butch had a resume he'd take a quick look at it and call him later in the week. Butch showed up at fifteen minutes before seven, five minutes before the owner arrived. This made a good impression. Butch gave his resume to the owner. The owner glanced at the resume, and then decided to stop and look it over more closely. One can only speculate that key information on the resume must have jumped out at the employer because he took a few moments to read the resume. The employer interviewed and hired Butch that day (with a provision that his references were verified).

The Information Available at a Glance

Let's look at what information was available at a glance on Butch's resume. In the heading, the nickname *Butch* appears in parentheses. This has several functions. Butch has almost never been called Roland. He's almost forgotten that *Roland* is his birth name. This means that if a potential employer calls for references to one of his old jobs, there is a chance the people they call may not know Butch's actual first name. A reference check for a Roland Stewart might come back with the reply, "No one by that name ever worked here, sorry." A statement like that would immediately end someone's possibilities for a job. This has actually happened.

Let's look at what may have influenced the owner of Landford Construction to hire Butch on the spot. In the Overview section, the word *Journeyman* means that Butch has a certain amount of expertise in his field. In all professions, certain key words carry a lot of power. The fact that Butch is a Journeyman in two fields not only speaks well for Butch, but also interests the owner of Landford, because the company does both acoustical ceilings and trim carpentry. The statement: *Management of employees* may or may not be important to Landford for the job position for which Butch is applying, however it does relay a level of responsibility. You won't always know all the needs of the company where you apply, but some items are good to list in case they are valuable to the company. That is why Butch listed his willingness to travel. Butch knows that some companies need workers to go to remote sites for jobs, and he wants Landford to know immediately how he feels about travel.

Butch liked the heading "Professional Experience" over "Work Experience" for his resume, even though he is a construction worker. Although Butch isn't a $250K a year executive, he is proud of what he does and the care he takes in his work.

At a glance, the owner of Landford can see that Butch has stayed at Reilly Acoustics for several years. In construction, some workers are not steady and dependable. Someone who stays for a long time is often a good prospect for employment. Most of the information about what Butch does is contained under Reilly. Not only is this the most recent work Butch has done, but Butch is applying for a comparable position at Landford (installing acoustical ceilings). His acoustical work is what is needed at Landford. The information in this area is brief and to the point. There is no elaboration. Discussion of items in detail are best left for an interview. Not much is said under Butch's other jobs. If Butch were applying for a trim carpentry position, his work experience for All Service Doors, WesTrim, and D&L would have more content and his work with acoustical ceilings would have less.

Butch had other jobs after graduating from high school before he worked in construction. Those jobs do nothing to add to his appeal for the job he is now seeking. He has such a solid work history in his field that those jobs on the resume would only result in their taking up valuable space. They would not enhance his attractiveness to an employer. A job history doesn't need to include every place a person has worked.

It isn't uncommon that carpenters do not graduate from high school so Butch has listed that he *is* a high school graduate. If he had graduated college, this wouldn't be necessary, because high-school graduation would be assumed. He has also listed other courses he's taken since high school. In today's competitive job market, extra education is always a plus. The owner of Landford Construction mentioned he liked Butch's willingness to participate in classes outside of work. The courses he took can easily be seen at a glance.

JOSEPH D. FISK

201 Westridge Dr.
Dallas, Texas 75356
Home: (972) 481-4499
Fisk@hotmail.com

OVERVIEW:

- Over seven years of experience as Networking Engineer.
- Strong Expertise in TCIP, Cisco Routers, ATM, and UNIX.
- Excellent communications skills at all levels, from Engineering Teams to Customers.
- Skilled at translating technology to understandable language for the laymen.

PROFESSIONAL EXPERIENCE:

Enterprise Systems — Dallas, TX   *1999 — Present*

* *Data Network Engineer*

- Inventoried and documented Qwest Communications' entire OSS network infrastructure.
- Built UNIX scripts to automate day-to-day activities and to query network equipment for statistics and configurations.
- Documented troubleshooting procedures and engineering specifications of their network infrastructure.

Warner Telecom — Greenwood Village, TX   *1995–1999*

* *Data Network Engineer (1998–1999)*

- Engineered and managed transition of Warner's entire core network infrastructure to new location with no down time while simultaneously improving network efficiency.
- Engineered, configured and managed installation of metropolitan area ATM networks using Xylan OmniSwitches and PizzaSwitches used to provide transparent LAN services to Warner Telecom customers.
- Designed and implemented a management platform using HP Openview Network Node Manager and Xylan XVision to provide alarm and remote provisioning capabilities into the NOC.
- Developed testing and troubleshooting procedures for this network.
- Designed and constructed an Intranet Web server to store and update all OSS engineering documentation using forms and C programs.
- Designed and implemented network security policies and procedures using router access lists and firewalls.

Joseph D. Fisk   *Page 2*

* *OSS Network Engineer (1995–1998)*

- Engineered and managed installation of nationwide OSS/IT network infrastructure.
- Configured and maintained OSS and IT networking equipment including high-end Cisco routers, Cisco FDDI/CDDI concentrators, Cisco Ethernet repeaters and switches, Xyplex terminal servers, and AI Switches.
- Maintained configuration documentation.
- Provided high level troubleshooting on router, frame relay, X.25, and TCP/IP problems.
- Implemented network security with router access lists and firewalls.
- Evaluated and optimized local and wide-area networks for capacity and speed.
- Coordinated with Network Applications Group for alarm visibility in the National Operations Center.
- Evaluated new vendor products such as ATM switches; Ethernet hubs; and switches, routers, and modems.

EDUCATION:

BS, Electrical Engineering, GPA 3.5, University of Texas, 1995

CERTIFICATIONS:

Cisco Certified Network Associate (CCNA)

TECHNICAL SKILLS:

Operating Systems:
UNIX (Solaris 2.x)
LINUX, Windows 95/98/2000
Windows NT Server/Workstation

Networking Equipment:
Cisco Routers—1600, 2500, 4000, 4500, 3600, and 7000 series.
Cisco ATM Switches—BPX
Cisco Ethernet Switches—Catalyst 2900 and 5000 series.
Cisco DSLAM—6100 and 6130
Copper Mountain DSLAM—CE200
N-Base (formerly Xyplex)—1620 and 1640 Terminal Servers and 9000 Chassis.
Applied Innovations—AI180, AI130, AIScout and AIM Chassis.
Alcatel (former Xylan equipment)—Omni 3, 5 and 9 Chassis.

ROLAND (BUTCH) STEWART

8570 First Street
Westminster, Colorado 80030
Home: (303) 428-9907

OVERVIEW:

- Journeyman in acoustical ceilings and wall panels with over twelve years of experience.
- Journeyman in trim carpentry with over eight years of experience.
- Management of employees.
- Job management responsibilities.
- Willing to do what it takes to meet deadlines.
- Willing to travel.

PROFESSIONAL EXPERIENCE:

Reality Acoustics—Denver, CO   *1988–Present*

* *Carpenter/Foreman*

Installation of acoustical grid and tile systems, specialty ceilings, and acoustical wall panels. Oversee workers' production and work quality. At times required to relocate for several weeks at a distant job site. Occasionally work swing or midnight shifts.

- Has worked 10-hour days, 7-days a week in order to complete a project.
- Supervision of other workers.
- Met job deadlines.
- Learned how to work with new materials.
- Equipment operated includes forklifts, hydraulic scissors lift, power tools, scaffolding, and a laser level.

All Service Doors—Longmont, CO   *1987–1988*

* *Installer/Interior Trim Carpenter*

- Installation of wood doors, metal doors, and trim finish carpentry.

Roland (Butch) Stewart   *Page 2*

WesTrim—Denver, CO   <u>1987</u>

* *Interior Trim Carpenter*

- Installation of doors, window trim, baseboards and kitchen cabinets. Supervised two other carpenters.

D&L Construction—Denver, CO   <u>1986</u>

* *Interior Trim Carpenter*

Sunwest Builders—Denver, CO   <u>1985</u>

* *Interior Trim Carpenter*

Celebrity Homes Inc.—Denver, CO   <u>1980–1984</u>

* *Wrap-up/Warranty Carpenter*

- Detailed incomplete and missing items prior to homeowner moving in. Performed miscellaneous warranty repairs.

EDUCATION:

High School Graduate, Westminster, Colorado, 1978.
Two Years Carpenter Apprenticeship at Construction Industry Training Council of Colorado, 1989 and 1990.
Blueprint Reading at Adult Education, Adams County, 1990.
Fundamentals of Supervision at Front Range Technical School, 1991.

Two Resumes: Which Candidate Do You Want To Interview?

Think of yourself as employer who wants to fill a position for a front office worker at a middle school. Take a look at the next two resume examples: Ann Evans on page 22, and Betty Barr on page 24. Decide which person you want to interview for the job.

An Analysis of the Ann Evans Resume

This resume obviously won't survive a fifteen-second read. If it gets a thorough reading, there are several major problems. The Objective tells us nothing. Since Ann sent the resume in to apply for a secretarial/clerical position, an employer already knows she is interested in getting the job. Stating her objective wastes an employer's reading time.

Skills and abilities contain long paragraphs that are tedious to read. The use of *I* on a resume is not recommended. The indentation of the text wastes precious space on a resume and the small font is difficult to read. Her Work History is missing. Its absence deprives the employer of valuable evaluation tool.

References don't belong on a resume, and neither does a statement about references being available. An employer assumes that references are available upon request. There is no header on page two so if the page become separated from page one, it cannot be matched up with the first page of the resume.

An Analysis of the Betty Barr Resume

The *overview* reads like the answers to a list of questions a potential employer might ask of someone applying for a school secretary position. Addressed are questions like: "Can you work well in a team atmosphere? Do you work well without supervision? Can you meet deadlines under time constraints even if you are interrupted often in a very busy office environment?" If Betty were applying for a job at the executive level, the information in the overview would take on a different emphasis as seen in Steve Anderson's resume. However, for this position, this overview works. The overview emphasizes the point that this person can do the job without making the employer deduce it from paragraphs of information listed in the work experience.

Her Work History listed under *Professional Experience* has her skills broken down into categories for the Golden Oaks job. Those categories make the information easy to understand at a glance. The bulleted area below each category offers details.

More than an Education category appears on page two. *Medical training* is important for a school office worker. That is listed clearly under its own heading so the potential employer knows that this person has the training, which may well give her an edge over other candidates. Knowing how to use office equipment and computer programs is also a concern for people applying for this position. Betty makes certain that information about her qualifications in these areas can be found quickly.

Even if an employer takes the time to read through a poorly organized resume, on subsequent reviews, or during an interview, key information that is buried in the test is often forgotten. This can result in someone less qualified getting the job.

The Ann Evans and Betty Barr Resumes Were Actually the Same Person

To make a point, the same person's resume was used in both examples. The Ann Evans version was the original resume and the Betty Barr sample was the version after using techniques in this book to revise the information. For the record, the Betty Barr version beat out a lot of competition. She not only got her interview, but she got the job. Looking at the resume in the Betty Barr form, it is easy to see she is qualified.

2949 Oakwood St.
Las Vegas, NV
Phone: 702-495-4464

Ann Evans

Objective To obtain a secretarial/clerical position with a district school.

Skills and Abilities **Communication/Listening:** Strong communicator with excellent verbal, written and listening skills. Carefully listen to what is being said and able to relay that information back to whomever it is intended. Good phone skills with ability to handle multiple lines. Work well with the public. Able to handle and clam down upset parent when needed. Can multi-task in the office setting. Inventory control & product ordering.

Classify Data: Managed all aspects of the filing process to include updating, tracking, purging, archiving, and merging of information. Ensure information is posted in a timely and accurate manner. Maintained over 350 students and employee records for a school. Assisted in the development of a student tracking system for attendance at Desert View Charter School.

Creative: Have an eye for layout and design of printed material. Like to brainstorm to make finished projects look their best. Produced various flyers, brochures, and other printed materials. Completed many photographic projects. Have assisted in production of school year book.

Dependable and Responsible: Have a reputation for being true to my word and meeting deadlines. Not afraid to ask questions on things I am unclear about. Often times in the past, I have been entrusted with sensitive information that required confidentiality and discretion in handling to protect the parties involved. Understand the issues of confidentiality regarding student records, special education issues, testing information/results, student and/or staff discipline.

Arranged Functions: Coordinated special functions, speakers and events. Perform all the follow up activities necessary to ensure the function runs smoothly. Have arranged accommodations, travel, meals, and the social gatherings for groups over 50 people, field trips, school pictures, special assemblies, after school activities.

Detail Oriented: Like to see assigned projects completed correctly. Think through my tasks, anticipating causes and effects of what I am involved in. Enjoy breaking down large projects into smaller more manageable sizes and ensuring nothing gets lost in the process. Learn from my mistakes to improve future projects.

Well Organized: Develop itemized lists when developing projects, keeping information clearly organized by subject. Have organized information in a sensible manner so others can easily follow intent and direction.

Locate Information: Enjoy researching different topics to obtain information to answer questions. I've begun with limited information many times and finished with valuable resources that were compiled for future reference. Example: Learning about standardized testing materials/assessment coordinator for CSAP testing for Charter School.

Other
In addition to having 3 children, ranging in ages from 10-16 years old; I have had many years in working with children and youth. Areas include director of a children's ministry department, teacher of preschoolers, and advising middle school age children. I am outgoing, energetic; promise to work hard and excited to learn new tasks and skills.

References
1. Linda Smith, 702-221-1077
2. Deborah Day, 702-231-0703
3. Janet Reno, 702-592-0360

BETTY BARR

2815 Smith Road
Denver, Colorado 80003
Home: (303) 881-1857

OVERVIEW:

- Work well in team atmosphere; good at working without direct supervision.
- Can multi-task in office setting.
- Successful at meeting deadlines under time constraints and with multiple interruptions in a busy office environment.
- Understand the issues of confidentiality regarding student records, special education issues, employee records, and discipline issues.
- Experienced in tactful handling of sensitive information that requires confidentiality and discretion to protect all parties involved.
- Work extremely well with the public. Effective communicator.
- Good phone skills. Used to handling multiple lines.
- Very detail oriented and well-organized.
- Experienced in administering medications and maintaining the appropriate documentation for the student.

PROFESSIONAL EXPERIENCE:

Golden Oaks Charter Academy — Denver, CO   *1997–Present*

* *Records/Clerical/Attendance Secretary*

Record Keeping Duties:
- Responsible for receiving, transferring, and archiving student and staff records.
- Maintain employee records.
- Responsible for maintaining and tracking employee leave.
- Contact, schedule, and track substitute teaching staff.
- Assist in maintaining purchasing records and data for school.

Administrative/Clerical Duties:
- Handle scheduling for standardized testing material.
- Handle public relations for school.
- Arrange field trips, special assemblies, and travel for teachers.
- Main resource for parent information, including school tours, answering questions about the facility, and curriculum.

Attendance and Other Duties:
- Track daily attendance of students. Contact parents regarding student absences.
- Help administer medications for students and maintain appropriate documentation for student medications.

Betty Bar *Page 2*

Chapel Hills Baptist Church—Arvada, CO   *1995–1997*
(Mom's Morning-Out Program)

* *Preschool Teacher*

Worked directly with young children in a positive environment.
- Created lesson plans and taught in preschool program.
- Administered medications when necessary.
- Filled in for administrative staff when necessary.

Photography Business   *1985–Present*

Started up and currently run a freelance photography business.
Responsible for all bookkeeping, records, and scheduling.

EDUCATION:

One year, Marketing/Management, Phillips College, Gulfport, MS, 1984
High School Diploma, Golden Springs High School, Golden Springs, CO, 1982

SPECIALIZED MEDICAL TRAINING:

CPR Certification
General First Aid

OTHER COURSES:

Marketing and Advertising Workshops
Various Photography Courses

OFFICE EQUIPMENT:

Multiple Phone Lines
Fax Machine
Various Copy Machines
Most Typical Office Equipment

COMPUTER PROGRAMS:

Microsoft Office
Excel
Microsoft Word

Chapter 3

Building Your Resume

> The resume can be broken down into five basic parts: heading, overview, work history, education, and special training and skills. This chapter shows how to construct each part.

HEADING

What is needed: Name, full address, phone numbers where you can be reached, and email address.

What is not needed: Fancy decorations, lettering too large in comparison with other information, your picture, more than one email address, the word *Resume*.

In general a good heading starts with the persons name on the first line, and has a space separating the name from the rest of the contact information. The name ideally is larger than the rest of the heading, but not obnoxiously so. Usually 14 point is a good size when the rest of the heading is 12 point. The heading is the first thing to appear on the resume and is presented in a logical order, which makes the information easy to access for the potential employer.

Example

Samuel R. Walker

3109 Marion Drive
Denver, Colorado 80030
Home: (303) 477-0149
Sam@aol.com

The above example looks fairly straightforward and simple. Some people may worry that it doesn't make them stand out from the rest of the crowd. A showy resume doesn't get people an interview. A professional looking resume that tells a potential employer that you have the skills and work history the employer is looking for is what gets the interview.

NAME

In the example, the name appears fairly straightforward, but there are rules that affect certain resumes.

Use of a Nick Name

If you have a nickname that people know you by that isn't commonly understood, state your nickname in the heading of the resume. Resumes are often used for reference checks. Too often, people with nicknames have lost a good reference due to confusion about names. For example, one salesman who everyone called Mick had a reference check called into a previous employer. The secretary flatly stated that they had never had a Mike Smith working for them, even though the secretary knew Mick fairly well. No one had ever called him by his real name. Here is how you can present that information:

Example

Mike (Mick) Smith

Titles and Degrees

If you are a CPA, and you are applying for an accounting job, use your title after your name. If you are a sergeant or lieutenant and you are applying for a non-military job, don't use your title after your name. Only use titles that are relevant to the job you are seeking.

If you have a Ph.D., use that designation after your name. Don't use the title *Dr.* in front of your name. That causes confusion with someone who is a medical doctor. Even medical doctors should not use *Dr.* and can more clearly state their profession as follows:

Example
Not This Way:

Dr. James T. Smith

This way:

James T. Smith, M.D.

Be sure to use a comma before the degree.

Birth Designations

Junior or numeric designations are used after a name as follows:

Example

Joe F. Smith III

Jack L. Walker Jr.

The correct way to state junior or senior is without a comma (as shown in the example above).

Middle Initials

Use of a middle initial has advantages. Some companies can receive resumes with identical names. If you have a common name, your name is likely to be duplicated. Duplications can leave you out of the running for an interview. Using a middle initial provides an employer with a way of differentiating two similar names.

Work Titles in a Heading

Work titles such as *Vice President* or *Sales Manager* should never appear in a heading.

ADDRESS

Typically there is just one address stated per resume. The most common exception is for college students. For the typical address, spell out *Court, Drive* and other address designations. Also spell out the state name. Do not use abbreviations for the state. The exception to this rule is if spelling out the state creates too large a heading that looks out of balance on the page.

Handling Dual Addresses

Students nearing graduation often need to state a dual address when sending out their resumes. The following example shows how that situation is handled.

Example

SCOTT BROOKS

Scott@aol.com

School Residence:	**Home Residence:**
224 Bracket Hall	**705 Fairview Ave.**
University of Colorado	**Monument, Colorado**
College Phone: 303-786-4062	**Home: 719-481-3872**

PHONE NUMBERS

One or more phone numbers are common and appropriate. Always label the phone number as *Home, Work* or *Cell*. Sometimes it is strategic to label a phone as *Evening* or *Daytime* in place of the word *Home*. State the home phone number first, the work second, and the cell last. Only state the work phone number if an interested employer can call without negative consequences for you at your current job. Some employees find their current jobs in jeopardy if they receive phone calls from potential employers at work.

Label *Home* and *Work* simply. The word *Home* followed by a colon is enough. The word *phone* following *Home* or *Work* is not necessary. People can tell by the format that the following is a phone number:

Example

Home: (505) 487-1452
Work: (505) 444-1221
Cell: (222) 458-1463

A good way to set off the area code is with parentheses. That style makes reading the phone number easier for someone who is dialing. Dashes are also acceptable. Cell phones need to be included if you are usually available during work hours at you cell phone number. Don't use periods to separate area code and phone prefix, because they make the phone number difficult to read when dialing.

EMAIL

More and more businesses are using email for communications. Some people respond quicker to email than to regular mailing. Be cautious when using a work email address. Some companies check work emails and will fire employees for using the email for personal reasons. The general rule of thumb is to only list one email address. Usually this is your home email. If you don't check that email often, while looking for a job, add that to your tasks rather than risk problems by listing a work email.

An email address doesn't need a label. People who are Internet literate will recognize an email address at a glance. Because email is newer to the communications world, it is traditionally listed last in the heading.

If you have a nonprofessional email address such as *Hipguy@aol.com*, you are wise to change the email address to a more professional one for your resume. Think of the impression you are making with the email address you use on your resume.

WHAT MAKES A POOR HEADING

- The information that belongs on one line appears on two lines. For example the city and state need to be on the same line as the zip code. Don't put the zip code on a new line.
- A very large name and the rest of the heading that is too small or is accented with decorative fonts. The result is contact information like the address and/or phone number that is difficult to read on the original and impossible to read on a faxed copy.
- Incomplete names (nicknames missing when appropriate, no middle initial with common names, only using initials in place of the first name). Incorrect name information (titles that are inappropriate or incorrectly stated).
- Incomplete phone numbers. Make sure you include your area code even if you are applying for a job in your local calling area. Some companies have offices outside of the local calling area and may need the complete information.
- Not listing a daytime phone number. Ideally the phone number you list is one at which you can easily be reached during work hours. If you can only list a home number, get an answering machine and make a habit of checking it during the day. Most machines allow remote access.

- Don't put a picture on the resume. Pictures cause several problems. They don't fax well and they can introduce information that causes a bias in hiring. Some companies will shy away from a resume bearing a picture.

The Overview Section
Although the Overview section appears next in the resume, since the information is dependant on work history, that subject is covered last in this chapter.

Professional Experience

Professional experience contains the work history of the resume. Included in the work history are the company name, dates of employment, title for position held, job duty descriptions, and accomplishments. On your resume, this section doesn't appear directly after the heading, but it is the part that needs to be assembled next. This area is where you will do your hardest work. At this point you will only type in raw material. Formatting for the final appearance of the resume is covered in Chapter 4.

> **In the work history, your most recent job always appears first.**

Company Name

The line which contains the company name includes the current name of the company, the city and state that the company is located in, and the dates you worked for the company. When stating the company name, if another company has recently acquired the company, use the *new* official company name. Initials representing a company are fine as long as they are readily identifiable outside of your company.

With some companies, you will want to include the designation of the company such as LLC (Limited Liability Company) or Inc. (Incorporated). The criteria is to use a company name that makes sense to the people who will read the resume. Be careful to use the entire title of the company. *Coors* isn't just Coors, it is actually *Coors Brewery*. Although around the plant everyone merely calls the place Coors, your resume is going to be read by people outside your regular work circle and must contain the complete and official name.

Example

<u>*Coors Brewery*</u>

not

<u>*Coors*</u>

> **Please note: Until you add formatting, the information you type will not appear the same as the samples in the book. Don't worry about the appearance of the raw information. The chapter on formatting will change the final appearance.**

City and State

The city and state where the company is located follows the company name on the resume. Abbreviate the state by using two capital letters.

Example

Coors Brewery — Golden, CO

Use a long dash (an em dash) to separate the name of the city from the name of the company. Chapter 4 tells you how to make an em dash. Use the two-letter abbreviation for the state. When using the two-letter abbreviation for the state, capitalize both letters, and do not use a period or any other punctuation. If the company is in a foreign country, you may need to spell out the entire country name to make sure the reader can easily identify it.

Year and Date of Employment

Work dates consist of the year you started working at the company and the last year you worked at the company. If you are employed at that company, use the word *present* in place of the current year. Using the current year instead of the word *present* implies you no longer work at the company, and have recently left.

For now, just use a tab between the state and your employment date. The chapter on formatting will tell you how to get the correct look for the final copy. Use an en dash (a medium length dash) between the start date and the final date.

Example

Coors Brewery — Golden, CO   1998–Present

In most cases, you can state the year you started working and not the month. An exception to this is if you have worked at two places within the same year. For those situations, separate the month with a slash as shown in the example below.

Example

Joe's Pizza — Cincinnati, OH   2/99–5/99

Martha's Fine Gifts — Dayton, OH   5/99–8/99

Stating the Division of a Company

At some companies, it is necessary to state a division name to clearly identify the place of employment. State the division first, and use a slash to separate the division name from the company name.

Example

Avalon Books/Division of Thomas Bouregy—New York, NY   *1999–Present*

Clarifying Company Names Involving Multiple Locations, Buyouts, Name Changes, and Mergers

Multiple Locations of the Same Company
If you are working for a company that has several locations, and you have worked at more than one of those locations, don't give a state next to the company name; instead, handle that information in the job title section.

Example
Incorrect:

Agilent Technologies—Colorado Springs, CO   *1995–Present*

* *Division Manager*

Agilent Technologies—Palo Alto, CA   *1978–1995*

* *Division Manager*

Correct:

Agilent Technologies   *1978–Present*

* *Division Manager, Colorado Springs, CO (1995–Present)*

* *Division Manager, Palo Alto, CA (1978–1995)*

> Note that although the example shows two job positions listed one after the other, on the actual resume these job positions would be separated by work history data. Don't state two job titles and then group all of the work information together, leaving the employer to wonder what you did where. An example of how this is done correctly is on page 36 under *Each Job Title Deserves its Own Work History*.

When you create your resume, you need to keep in mind that a lot of information will be only skimmed. At a glance, the incorrect way (shown above) makes it appear as if the employee has worked at two different companies instead of two different locations in the same company. The unwanted result is that an employer may think that this employee only worked a few years at each of two companies as opposed to having worked at Agilent for seventeen years, and in fact was valuable enough to transfer to another state. Use the correct style to keep your work history absolutely clear.

Buyouts, Name Changes, and Mergers

Companies go through buyouts, name changes, and mergers. For employees, making the change is sometimes difficult. You need to put any feelings aside when creating a resume. Look at the resume from the perspective of the reader who doesn't necessarily remember the way things were before a change occurred. When creating a resume, the most recent name needs to be listed even if the company is better known by its former name. To help a resume reader better identify the company you worked at, a small explanation helps. The place for that explanation is either directly under or following the company name. Keep any additional material strategic, short, and relevant.

Example

Agilent Technologies — Palo Alto, CA   *1978–2001*
(Formerly Hewlett Packard)

Sometimes it is of value to elaborate on the name explanation.

Example

Agilent Technologies — Palo Alto, CA   *1978–2001*
(Agilent Technologies spun off from Hewlett Packard in 1999)

or:

KABCO Toys — Reno, NV   *1995–Present*
(KABCO bought out Wonderland Toys in 2000)

or:

Goodwill Printing — Pasco, WA   *1990–2002*
(Goodwill Printing bought out Joe's Print Shop in 2001 and closed it down in 2002)

Some name changes can be explained on the same line with the company name. Usually space is the determining factor.

Example

Wonder Toys (Formerly Child's Dream) — Pasco, WA   *1977–1999*

After a few years, the general population knows buyouts, mergers, and name changes for companies, or the significance is lost completely. If a company listed on your resume was bought out after you left, you need to reflect the current name of the company on your resume. The rule of thumb is to list the same name the receptionist uses when answering the phone.

When to Describe the Business

At times, there are advantages to giving a brief description of the company where you worked. For example, if you are the manufacturing manager applying to a similar sized company, there is an advantage in stating that you've had specific experience with running that size plant.

Example

Smith Printing Company — East Greenville, PA   *1987–2002*
A $60M division of Quick Speed Printing. Smith Printing specializes in printing monthly magazines ranging in circulation from 60,000 to 100,000.

Information in this section can include clarification of the company's business if it is not revealed by the company name. For instance *Joe's Autos* doesn't tell you that Joe specialized in antique automobiles. If you are applying to a garage that also specializes in antiques, that is relevant information. If you are not applying to an auto repair shop that specializes in antiques, leave that information out. The use of parentheses is optional.

Example

Joe's Auto Shop — East Greenville, PA   *1987–2002*
(Joe's Auto Shop specializes in rejuvenation of rare and antique automobiles.)

Information you can use to describe a company includes:

- The size of the company.
- The specialty of the company when it is not clearly revealed by the name alone.
- Key words that point out similarities between a company on your resume and the company you are applying to (when the company name doesn't reveal that information).
- The Fortune 500 or Fortune 100 rating if you are applying to a company that has a similar rating.
- A company that the general public associates with a specific kind of work, but where you did a different kind of work. Sometimes a division at the company where you are applying does the specialty work.

What doesn't belong:

- Information describing a company where you only worked for a short time.
- Information about a company you worked for a long time ago.
- Information about a company that most people immediately recognize and whose market share is well known. For example, you don't need to explain IBM. The general population knows about the business.

In general, make any information you add immediately below the company name relevant to your position at that company and relevant to the job for which you are applying. Any information included must have a strategic advantage or you waste precious resume space and the resume reader's time.

Job Title

The job title must make sense to the resume reader and accurately reflect what you did. Many businesses use similar job titles throughout an industry. For example, a Sales Representative is commonly known as someone who sells products. It is clear to most individuals what a Human Resource Manager does and the term Personnel Manager is readily interchangeable in most people's minds with Human Resource Manager. Use the job title you had when you worked in the position. Doing that makes you more traceable when people call for references. However, be aware that it can create a problem on your resume if your company uses unique titles that are only fully understood within the company. For example, if your customer service position is more like another company's sales representative position, you may need to include both titles to make your talents clear at a glance.

Example

* *Customer Service/Sales Representative*

With some job positions, the skills and job descriptions are not well understood throughout the industry. For these jobs there are two options: The first is if the job information that follows the title clears up the uncertainties, then the job title can stand as stated. The second is with a title like Resources Engineer, where many employers may not know this job is similar to the job opening. In these cases, include additional information to make the job title meaning more clear. This can be done by stating the company's title for the job, and then in parentheses stating a more recognizable job title.

Example

* *Resources Engineer (Maintenance Man)*

Working Two Jobs at the Same Time

If you are working two jobs at the same time, put the most important job first. Jobs worked simultaneously need not be presented together. For example, a concurrent job may be listed last on the resume when it is insignificant or is a home office position. At other times, the simultaneous job is omitted altogether.

Presenting One Position at a Company

If you worked at only one position in a company, the date information appears on the same line as the company.

Example

<u>*Quill Publications—New Haven, CT*</u>   <u>*1996-1999*</u>

* *Editing and Layout*

- Laid out articles and ads for magazine and book publications.
- Edited both content and grammar of copy prior to publication.
- Transcribed audio interviews for article publication.
- Sized and retouched photos for printing.

Presenting Multiple Positions at a Company

If you work at more than one position, or at more than one location, list the total years worked at the company on the company line; then use the space after the job title for telling how long you worked at each position. The job title can also be used to state different locations you worked at while you were employed at a company. The work dates at each position, division, or location goes in parenthesis after the job title. Of course, each job title needs to be followed by its accomplishments as stated below.

Each Job Title Deserves its Own Work History

A common mistake made by people working in several positions at one company is to list all the job titles together followed by a single job description and list of accomplishments. This type of presentation doesn't give the employer a solid feel for how you performed and progressed in each position. That is a disadvantage. Often people who do this kind of grouping fail to show many accomplishments at all. The resume needs to be written to clearly represent who you are and what you did. Take a look at the following example. The first example groups the job titles together and then groups the accomplishments and job information together. The second example does it the correct way.

Example
Incorrect:

<u>*Smith Printing—Waterloo, WI*</u>   <u>*1978-1995*</u>

* *Pre-Press Supervisor (1990–1995)*
* *Customer Service Representative (1987–1990)*
* *Image Assembler/Management Trainee (1978-1987)*

- Managed the accounts of ten other CSR's, including all customer contact, and final responsibility for all products coming off of 11 web offset presses. This was the final checkpoint for millions of press impressions each day.
- Responsible for estimating any potential new customer work.
- Developed archive system for managing the storage and retrieval of files used in the production of JC Penney catalogs.
- Produced over 9,000 plates per month.
- Trained in all areas including manufacturing and corporate departments.

- Scheduling, inventory, vendor contact, billing, hiring, employee relations and general troubleshooting.
- Supervised a commercial prepress department with 70+ employees in a union environment. Product mix included *Time, People, Sports Illustrated*, and *Business* magazines.

If you have nothing but time on your hands, see if you can figure out which bullets go with each position in the example above. If you succeed, it will take you a lot longer than a potential employer will be willing to spend.

Example
Correct:

Smith Printing — Waterloo, WI   *1978–1995*

* *Pre-Press Supervisor (1990–1995)*

- Smith Printing is a $300M printer with headquarters in Waterloo, WI. This position included scheduling, inventory, vendor contact, billing, hiring, employee relations, and general troubleshooting.
- Supervised a commercial prepress department with 70+ employees in a union environment. Product mix included *Time, People, Sports Illustrated*, and *Business* magazines.
- Produced over 9,000 plates per month.
- Responsible for estimating any potential new customer work.
- Developed archive system for managing the storage and retrieval of files used in the production of JC Penney catalogs.

* *Customer Service Representative (1987–1990)*

- Managed the accounts of ten other CSR's, including all customer contact, and final responsibility for all products coming off of 11 web offset presses. This was the final checkpoint for millions of press impressions each day.

* *Image Assembler/Management Trainee (1978-1987)*

- Trained in all areas, including manufacturing and corporate departments.

Clarify Generic Job Titles

Make sure the job title explains what the job entails. One of the most common generic titles is the title of Vice President. For some companies, this title represents one set of duties. For others, there may be twelve Vice Presidents, one for sales, one for manufacturing, one for marketing and so on. The title Vice President doesn't give a clear idea of job duties. If there is doubt about job duties related to a specific title, make sure you include a short paragraph that describes the job duties before you list your accomplishments.

Work Description

Work history is the part of the resume that portrays who you are and what you have done. Although it is fine to put down all you want to about what you've done at a particular position, you will need to shape the work history before you send off the resume. Different jobs may require different shaping of the resume.

> Each work history needs to be shaped by editing and tight-writing to target the job and the employer.

For a work history to be successful, you must cover pertinent information without extra words. Resume readers have both time limitations and attention-span limitations. The work history needs to be constructed dynamically or it can lose its effect. The job history is the part of the resume where you will work the hardest.

Researching Your Work Position

About yourself:
Know your field of work. Find out all about the kind of work you do. Join professional organizations if possible. Network with others doing similar work. Check newspaper ads for similar positions. How do they describe your work requirements? What do they see as important?

Researching Where You Are Sending the Resume

Look at job requirements listed by the company you want to apply to. Also look into the company to which you plan to send the resume. Learn what that company is all about by searching the Internet for information, by reading brochures that are available from the company, or by making a phone call to talk to the receptionist at the company.

Brainstorming Session

After you've done your research, sit down and brainstorm. Write a job description for your replacement at your current job. List what you do on a daily, weekly, and monthly basis. If you have yearly requirements, jot those down, too. Think about what skills are needed for this job. Search your memory for any and all accomplishments you've made. Don't worry about the volume of information. This is just a brainstorming session. You will refine the material later.

Cross Match Information

Now examine what you have written down from your brainstorming session. Compare your list to what the company is looking for in an applicant. Make sure all skills and accomplishments that match what the company is looking for appear on your resume. If this is a generic resume, use a consensus of job requirements from job ads for positions similar to the position you want.

The Ideal Work History Checklist

- Experience: Start with your most current job.
- Only show years worked. Do not show months.
- Give a short description of your responsibilities unless the job title will easily be understood by the resume reader.
- Present accomplishments and highlights about the job in bullets.
- The amount of resume space used for each job description and accomplishments should emphasize the importance of the different job positions. That importance needs to be tailored to include the accomplishments that match the company needs for the job position it is filling.
- Job descriptions and accomplishments are ideally the strongest in the most recent job and the jobs where you worked the longest.

Work History Believability

After the work history is finished, you need to step back and review the material. Be sure the information in the work history makes sense. As stated previously, the most recent job often has the most information. The exception is if you have only been there a short time. Many accomplishments at companies where you worked only a short time are not believable.

Job History Shaping

Typically the job at which you worked the longest has a respectable share of the accomplishments listed. The exception is if the job is in a different field from the job for which you are applying, or if you worked at the job a long time ago.

Jobs that are not related to your field should either be eliminated or only represented by job title and company name. If you need to show steady employment, present jobs outside your field briefly. If jobs outside your field are at the beginning of your work history, eliminate them altogether.

Is your job history contained within the first two pages? The overview, job history, and education ideally all need to be contained within one or two pages. If you have a large number of technical skills to list, a third page containing that information is acceptable. If you find your job history spilling over, go back and edit. Remember, just because you write it does not mean it will be read.

Hourly and Salary Resumes Sometimes Differ

Some hourly workers may not have a lot of accomplishments to list. Often their resumes consist mostly of a description of job responsibilities. If the information is fairly brief, a short paragraph may be used. If the information exceeds a short paragraph, use bullets or a combination of paragraph and bullets.

Example
Work History for an Hourly Job:

<u>*The Dog Works — Arvada, CO*</u>   <u>*2000–Present*</u>

* *Dog Groomer*

- Groom all breeds of dogs for both pet owners and for conformation classes.
- Familiar with grooming standards of all the major breeds.
- Responsible for booking clients and handling cash transactions.
- Deal directly with clients.
- Pick up and delivery of pets for elderly.
- Travel to four major dog shows to participate in on-site grooming.
- Designed newspaper ads and cards for business promotion.

> Make sure you list all pertinent tasks you did on a job. Sometimes a phone call can help you find out what is important in the job you hope to fill. With hourly jobs, anytime you can list accomplishments, that is always a plus.

Example of an Hourly Job Work Experience Refined from Raw Material to Resume:

> Below is shown information from the resume that appeared in Chapter 2 as the Ann Evans resume. The final form appeared as the Betty Barr resume. The original resume was more like raw data similar to what can be obtained from a brainstorming session. The following shows how the information was organized and rewritten to be more clear.

Organizing Brainstorming Material Into a Resume

The following was listed under the work history:

Communication and listening skills: Excellent verbal and written skills. Able to readily information back to whomever it is intended. Good phone skills. Ability to handle multiple lines. Able to calm down parents and students when needed.

Data skills: Filing, updating files, tracking files, purging, archiving and merging information. Insure information is posted in a timely and accurate manner. Maintained over 250 student and employee records for a school. Assisted in the development of school tracking system.

Creative: Have an eye for layout and design of printed material. Like to brainstorm to make finished projects look their best. Have produced flyers, brochures, and other printed material. Have worked with printer for final product. Have assisted in production of school yearbook.

Dependable and Responsible:
Have reputation for being true to word. Meet deadlines. Have been entrusted with sensitive information and upheld confidentiality and discretion with parties involved. Understands confidentiality regarding student records, and special education issues. Testing information and results. Student and staff discipline issues.

Arranged Functions: Coordinated special functions, speakers and events. Perform all the follow-up to make sure function ran smoothly. Have arranged accommodations, travel, meals, and social gatherings for groups over 50 people. Field trips, school pictures special assemblies and after school activities.

Detail Oriented: Like to see assigned projects completed correctly. Think through tasks, anticipating causes and effects of what I am involved in. Enjoy breaking down large projects into smaller more manageable sizes and ensuring nothing gets lost in the process. Learn from my mistakes.

Well Organized: Develop itemized lists when developing projects, keeping information clearly organized by subject. Have organized information in a sensible manner so others can easily follow intent and direction.

Locate information: Enjoy researching different topics to obtain information to answer questions. Have begun with limited information many times and finished with valuable resources that were complied for future references. Example-learned about standardized testing materials/assessment coordinated for CSAP testing for a charter school.

Other: Have experience with own children and other youth including children's ministry department in church. Have assisted with preschool and middle school teaching for Sunday school. Am outgoing, energetic, hard worker, and excited to learn new tasks and skills.

An Evaluation of the Raw Material

There is a lot of raw material and it is a little boring. Putting all of this information on a resume will almost guarantee the resume will not be read with any interest. To help make the information more interesting, it needs to be organized, made brief and to the point, shown as work and/or accomplishments done on the job, and easy to read.

The Information Reorganized for the Resume

Often, organizing and categorizing information helps with the presentation of a lot of dry material.

Example

Lewisville Charter Academy — Woodwork, PA   *1997–2000*

* *Records/Clerical/Attendance Secretary*

Record Keeping Duties:
- Responsible for receiving, transferring, and archiving student and staff records.
- Maintained employee records.
- Responsible maintaining and tracking employee leave.
- Contact, schedule and track substitute teaching staff.
- Assisted in maintaining purchasing records and data for school.

Administrative/Clerical Duties:
- Handled scheduling for standardized testing material.
- Handled public relations for school.
- Arranged field trips, special assemblies, and travel for teachers.
- Main resource for parent information, including school tours, answering questions about the, facility and curriculum.

Attendance and Other Duties:
- Tracking daily attendance of students, contacting parents regarding student absences.
- Helped administer medications for students and record appropriate documentation for student medications.

**Chapel Methodist Church,**   **_1995–1997_**
**(Mom's Morning-Out Program)**

* _**Preschool Teacher**_

Handled working directly with young children in a positive environment.
- Created lesson plans and taught in preschool program.
- Administered medications when necessary.
- Filled in for administrative staff when necessary.

> This takes the important parts of the information from the original resume and gives it relevance in a working situation. Some of the information can also be grouped into special skills areas and highlighted in the overview. Reading the example for the resume is much easier than plowing through the raw material. Unfortunately, too many resumes are sent out in a raw, unedited form.

Use of Paragraphs Instead of Bullets

Both regular paragraphs and bullets are effective in communicating information. If a paragraph form is used, the information must be easily understood, brief, and easy to skim through. Some resume readers feel that using bullets is the only way to convey information and is easier to read. Typically, employers will skim through a well-organized resume that uses paragraphs without hesitation.

Paragraphed Information

For people who prefer to convey information using a paragraph, below is an example of how to use a paragraph effectively.

Example

**National Sales Executive (1998–Present)** responsible for traditional catalog sales and "innovation" sales of highly versioned, database-driven direct mail programs. In 1999, earned the Highest Attainment to Budget Award nationally and the Salesperson of the Year award for the Midwest region. Yearly volume is in excess of $8M.

Resumes for Salaried Jobs

White-collar jobs often require more of an employee than just fulfilling the responsibilities of the job. These workers are expected to excel, create, produce and get results. With this kind of a resume you need to reflect what sets you apart from the competition, including what you accomplished in your previous job positions.

The Importance of Accomplishments

With salary or white-collar jobs, the accomplishments are the major emphasis on the resume. Never make a list of accomplishments without letting the employer know where you made the accomplishments. Accomplishments should be presented on a resume following the job title and any job description. They should never be grouped in their own separated area leaving an employer to guess at which job position these accomplishments were made.

Example
Accomplishments for a Job:

<u>*Laser Quill — Itasca, IL*</u>   <u>*1994–Present*</u>

*   *Sales Representative*

Represents all production services to the catalog, inserts, direct mail, magazine, and commercial client base for web offset and rotogravure printing, as well as auxiliary service such as material procurement, prepress, paper and mailing services.

- Responsible for selection and maintenance of outside vendor relationships for outsourcing services. Coordinate advertising and design agency activity.
- Selected as coordinating team member during corporate restructuring.
- Assisted in the design of Windows-based estimating and job control application, including enterprise-wide user training.
- Responsible for development and implementation of marketing strategies and fiscal goals. Provide client consultation per market trends and emerging technologies.
- Facilitated development and maintenance of national client database resulting in 30% increase in sales in 2001.
- Developed new markets resulting in $8M new sales in 2000 working with the printing department to design a more effective sales brochure.
- Developed largest amount of new business in the region for 1998 with a growth of 25% above sales target.

The introductory paragraph describes the kind of printing sales this person is involved with. The bullets present accomplishments at the job.

Using Only Bullets for Job Descriptions

Merely making a list of duties can accurately portray some job positions.

Example

Cleaner Homes—Toledo, OH   *1997–2001*

* *Assistant Manager*

- Scheduled workers for house cleaning.
- Managed employee problems.
- Total financial and accounting responsibility, including accounts payable, accounts receivable, general ledger entries, and payroll.
- Complete charge of business when manager out of town.

Bullet Guidelines

- Bulleted information is often not presented in complete sentences, but bulleted items need periods.
- The words *I* and *me* are never used.
- Use the active voice and start with action words. For example instead of "Workers were scheduled by me for house cleaning on a weekly basis." use "Scheduled workers for house cleaning."
- The information presented in the bullets is succinct and has no extra and unnecessary phrases. Job information that doesn't add value is dropped.
- Bulleted information needs to make sense to readers.

Let someone read your bulleted items to make sure that your sentences are not too fragmented to understand and that the sentence content makes sense to someone outside your work group. Also, don't put too much in one bulleted item. For example "Developed, wrote, and worked with a third-party production group to publish a service manual for the 55100 oscilloscope to include a separate manual for a U.S. Army/Navy special option." is too long. A better way to state the information is "Worked with an affiliated company to develop, write, and publish the service manual for the 55100 oscilloscope. Included was a separate manual for U.S. Army/Navy 'special option' requirements." There is no argument that the separate manual for US Army/Navy special requirements is very important. People with experience working with and for government establishments have a greater appeal to some employers. However, the information makes more sense to other readers when it is broken up and clarified.

A List of Dos for Work History

- Present the current job in present tense. Present all other jobs in the past tense. If you don't feel you can write in the present tense consistently, put all the job history in the past tense.
- Give the most current job the most emphasis. The emphasis is shown by more detail and more information. The exception is if you have only been at your current job a short

time or are applying for a job substantially different from the most recent job. In that case, put a lot of emphasis on the previous job with a longer work history or a previous job similar to the job you seek to obtain.

- Use material that is relevant to the job you are seeking. This may require you to have several versions of your resume for use when applying to different employers. That process is facilitated in this book because of the formatting techniques presented in Chapter 4.

- Be sure to address any skills you have that the potential employer is looking for. With some jobs, a statement like "scheduling workers" is a significant part of the job. For other jobs, that information needs to be left off. You need to scrutinize what is important with regard to the job for which you are applying.

- Keep information easy to read and to the point. A resume relays highlights, not insignificant details.

- Be sure to list your accomplishment under the name of the company where you made those accomplishments, especially when those accomplishments are noted in the overview.

- For less recent jobs, include less or no work details. Likewise, for jobs held outside your targeted job, less or little work details are needed.

- Arrange bulleted information strategically. Sometimes strategically is chronologically; sometimes it is the most important accomplishment first. Usually, it means putting like items together.

A List of Don'ts for Work History

- Don't be too general when you describe your accomplishments and job skills. For example, a sales representative can have great sales figures, but a resume reader also wants to know how those figures were attained, what kind of product was sold, and where the product was sold. Give relevance to job highlights with significant details.

- Don't be repetitious with job descriptions. If you said it clearly in a more recent job description, refer to that information and spend more text on accomplishments. You can repeat similar accomplishments at different jobs, to show a solid track record, but put the most detail with the most recent accomplishments and diminish the detail in successive job positions.

- Vary your sentences. Don't start each sentence with the same action word.

Example

- Responsible for the development of the 281-product line.
- Responsible for writing the manuals for three new scopes and introducing the product to the field.

Better:

- Developed the 281-product line (The 281 scope is a new high-frequency scope and its accessories led the market for two years).
- Wrote the manuals for three new scopes and introduced the product to the field.

Guidelines for Work History Format

- Spell out numbers *one* through *ten*. For numbers over ten, use numerals. Example: Managed 10,000 employees. Directly supervised three sales representatives.
- Use *million* and *billion* in place of zeros. Example: 23 million or 2.5M in place of 23,000,000. When quoting dollar amounts, round off the number. Don't write *$24,015* but do write *$24,000*.
- Don't use both the dollar sign and the word *dollar*. It is preferable to use the dollar sign. Example: $5 million or $5M or five million dollars. Not $5 million dollars. Note that the numeral catches people's attention more quickly than the amount written out in words. The same rule applies for percent. *3%* or *three percent*, not *3% percent*.
- For information presented in a series, use a comma. Also, use the comma to separate the last item in that series just prior to the word *and*. Example: Scheduled all performance evaluation workshops, supervisory training courses, and Toastmaster International meetings.
- Be sure to include a period at the end of sentences in bulleted lists. Periods may be excluded with very short lists consisting of a few words, but not sentences even if those sentences are sentence fragments.
- Don't use & in place of the word *and*. Example of *incorrect* usage: Have taken master water-skiing, scuba diving & water rescue courses.
- Don't mix spelled-out states and two letter abbreviations when stating the company locations. Use the two-capital letter abbreviation without a period, not the upper case and lower case abbreviation with a period.
- Never right justify the text.
- Although the information in bulleted lists is often short, to the point, and in sentence fragments, be sure that what is said makes sense to someone outside of the company. Have a friend read the information and flag areas that aren't clear.
- Ideally, the work history for each job should diminish in size from the most recent job to the earliest job listed.
- More is not better. What is better is a clear, accurate, and to-the-point picture of who you are and what you can do in the workplace.

More on Repetition and Quantity

Repetition of material needs to be a strategic decision. For example, repeating the key work areas for the job you are applying for supports the fact that you have many years of experience in the field. Repetition of accomplishments at different positions and higher positions shows you are a consistent achiever. Detailed repetition of a job description, however, is a poor use of space. Detailed repetition is when sentences are repeated word-for-word under different job titles. These sentences do not enlighten the resume reader about your job skills. A better way to present the information is to give the details about the job duties under the first job title, and then refer to that information in subsequent job descriptions where appropriate.

Work History Example and Critique of the Information

Example

<u>*Perfection, Inc. — Philadelphia, PA*</u>   <u>*1992–Present*</u>

* *Vice President Operations (1997–Present)*

Responsible for all North American Flexible Packaging business with five business unit leaders in three locations and over $70M in revenue. Responsible for company P&L.
- Turned an operation loosing $2M annually to profitability in seven months.
- Constructed and staffed a new business unit.
- Established key measures for service and quality in two new locations.
- Successfully integrated all business into the same computerized order entry and production systems.
- Began the development and application of statistical tools to the new processes.
- Awarded the Shinto Prize for Manufacturing Excellence in 1999.

* *Business Unit Leader (1993–1996)*

Overall P&L responsibility for a $20M coated products business.
- Improved service from 60% on time delivery to customers to 98%.
- Developed and implemented short run a strategic plan that generated double market growth and maintained marginal income despite material costs.
- Led a team that developed and implemented a supplier certification process.

* *Operations Manager (1992–1993)*

- Eliminated over $1M in cost over runs in one year.
- Negotiated successful labor agreements with Teamsters and GCIU leadership.
- Developed a manufacturing awareness and training program for all plant personnel.

<u>*Label World — Omaha, NE*</u>   <u>*1979–1992*</u>

* *Manufacturing Manager (1984–1992)*

Overall control of manufacturing operation for an $80M label, coating and converting operation in a multi-plant environment. Responsible for 12 direct reports and over 350 hourly employees.
- Improved on-time deliveries 35%.
- Improved order processing time 28%.
- Reduced total inventory 20% without affecting production.
- Reduced quality complaints 55%.

* *Production Manager (1982–1984)*

* *Materials Manager (1979–1982)*

This work history shows a pattern with this employee. This person is a successful manager who turns around losses, reduces costs, and increases production and quality. More detail about how the person achieved these accomplishments appears under the more recent jobs. Less recent jobs have just a brief listing of accomplishments. Whatever this person did as a Production Manager from 1982 to 1984 and a Materials Manager from 1979 to 1982 isn't significant enough to include in the resume when those accomplishments are compared to more recent job accomplishments so no details are given. A resume reader can still see that this person worked his or her way up in the company and tends to stay at a company for a long time. This person had a job prior to 1979, but that job did nothing to add value to the resume and was omitted. Also, anything done prior to 1979 is close to twenty-five years old which adds to its lack of significance. This is a good place to end the job history section for this resume.

Only One Company in a Work History

Some people have only one relevant job to list. For example, twenty years ago they got out of high school or college, maybe had an insignificant job for a while, and then went to work for a company where they stayed for many years. Within that company, they probably made progression from one area and/or level to another. For these people's resumes, listing only one company is not a problem. Don't hesitate to leave off employment during college unless it is part of your current profession. If the one job has a substantial number of years, miscellaneous jobs add nothing to your value as a potential employee.

Education

With few exceptions, you need to have an education area on your resume. This area typically follows the Work History and includes formal education such as high school and college.

College Degrees

Present information about college degrees briefly, logically, and completely. A good format to follow includes listing the kind of degree, the field the degree is in, the college where the degree was obtained, the city and state of the college, and the year you graduated. Separate all items by commas. The end of the line can have a period or it can be omitted; be sure to be consistent.

Example

BS, Chemistry, Metropolitan State College, Denver, CO, 1988.

This line says the person has a Bachelor of Science degree in chemistry which was received from Metropolitan State College in Denver, Colorado in 1988. That is often enough information for an employer. What isn't necessary is the word degree after the initials BS. The period at the end of the line is optional. (Note that some people prefer to present degrees with periods after each initial, such as *B.S.* Either way is acceptable.)

Regardless of how long ago you received your degree, you need to include the date you finished that degree. Give only the year you graduated and not the range of years you attended.

More Than One Degree

When you have more than one degree, list the highest level first.

Example

MS, Biochemistry, Metropolitan State College, Denver, CO, 1992.
BS, Chemistry, Metropolitan State College, Denver, CO, 1988.

Elaborating About a Degree

Sometimes it is of value to elaborate about a degree. If the extra information doesn't directly affect your suitability for the position, leave it out no matter how proud you are about the accomplishment. Everything in the resume needs to be tailored to the job for which you are applying. Keep in mind that the reader has an already-exhausted attention span because he or she probably reviewed a stack of resumes. Any extra information needs to be short and to the point. The following extra information is valuable for someone applying for a job in advertising.

Example

BA, Journalism (with emphasis in Advertising for Radio and Television), minor in Business Marketing, University of Phoenix, Tulsa, OK, 1990.

College Studies Without a College Degree

Sometimes a college education doesn't result in a degree. The uncompleted college education still needs to be listed.

Example

Three years towards a BA in Manufacturing Sciences, University of Washington, Seattle, WA, 1992–1995.

Currently attending Northwestern University's Kellogg Business School Executive MBA program.
BA, Business and Marketing, University of Washington, Seattle, WA, 1995.

Postgraduate studies in labor relations and bargaining practices, Cornell University, Buffalo, NY, 1987.
BS, Business, University of Cincinnati, Cincinnati, OH, 1984.
AA, Managerial Accounting, Cincinnati State College, Cincinnati, OH, 1980.

In general, if you went to college, always mention it no matter how long ago you went. If your college education is relevant, make sure the important parts are stated. If your college education has nothing to do with the job you are applying for, keep its description brief. Always include the area of a degree or study, even if it doesn't apply to the current job.

High School and Other Education

Because you need to have a high-school diploma or the equivalent to attend college, it is not necessary to state that you have a high-school education if you list any kind of college attendance. However, if you don't have any college education, and you do have a high-school diploma, state that information. Also list any pertinent adult education classes taken outside of high school. Because not all adult or special education courses taken after high school require a high-school diploma, be sure to include information about your high-school diploma if you have one.

Example

Blueprint Reading, Adult Education, Adams County, CO, 1990.
Two Years Carpenter Apprenticeship at Construction Industry Training, Council of Colorado, 1989 and 1990.
High School Graduate, Westminster High School, Westminster, Colorado 1978.

Special Training and Skills

Some courses are short, study courses. If they are relevant to the job for which you are applying, include them. If they are not relevant, a short statement instead of a list of courses can show that you readily take courses outside of work, and that the details don't relate to the position you are seeking.

Example

SPECIAL COURSES:

Public Speaking, On-Line Classes Inc., 1998
Becoming a Team Leader, On-Line Classes Inc., 1996
Group Dynamics in the Work Place, On-Line Classes Inc., 1994

Listing computer skills is usually a good idea, regardless of what position you are seeking. Some people in the workplace still resist using computers and this causes difficulty for their employers. If you have some computer competency, be sure to mention it.

Example

COMPUTER PROGRAMS:

Microsoft Office including Microsoft Word and Excel
Internet Searches and Email
ECHO—A Custom Database Program

Summarizing Skills and Equipment

For some resumes, even if the equipment used for a job is mentioned in the work history, it is extremely valuable to again sum it up in a quick and easy reference section. A lot of resume readers look for these lists of skills when trying to cut down on the resumes they will read more thoroughly.

Example

TECHNICAL SKILLS:

Programming Languages: Informix-4GL, Informix-SQL, FOCUS, SQL, COBOL, VSAM, QMF, FILEAID, REXX, EXEC
Databases: Informix, DB2, FOCUS, Stratagem
Editors: VI, ISPF, XEDIT
PC Software Applications: MS Word, MS Excel
Operating Systems: UNIX (DG, Sun), MVS, TSO, VM, Windows, DOS

OFFICE EQUIPMENT:

Multiple Phone Lines
Fax Machine
Various Copy Machines
Most Typical Office Equipment

Special Training

Special training also needs to be broken out into its own section on a resume when it applies to the job. If it doesn't apply to the job you are seeking, don't include it.

Example

TRAINING:

Oracle class, Pikes Peak Computer Training, 2000
Management Training, Dale Hall Specialty Classes, 1998

For training classes, unlike college education, the state in which the class was taken is not important. Just list the name of the class, the organization that held the class, and the year you took it.

Medical and Miscellaneous Skills

Listing medical abilities can be helpful to your resume such as first-aid training. If there is room, include these. Also mention any extra skills which would enhance your performance in the job, such as CPR training when you want to work at a school. Any security clearances are also important to include.

Accreditations/Affiliations

When they support your suitability for the job for which you are applying, accreditations, and affiliations should be mentioned in their own section.

The following list shows sections that are appropriate for some resumes. If any of these apply to your skills and are applicable to the job for which the resume is created, use them or something similar.

- Awards and Patents
- Board Membership
- Computer Skills
- Computer Software/Hardware Experience
- Courses
- Equipment
- Other Relevant Information
- Professional Activities
- Professional Awards
- Professional Development
- Professional Publications
- Professional Training
- CPA memberships, Toastmasters, club memberships that have significance to the job. Similar to information with Accreditations/Affiliations.

Overview

Why Resume Readers Want To See an Overview

Resume readers appreciate a well-constructed overview section. Even an easy-to-skim-through resume requires extra work on the reader's part to draw certain conclusions about the overall work history and how things in the skills area may affect the person's achievements. For example, if an employee has worked at the most recent company for ten years as a manager, and worked at his previous company for ten years, during five of which he was a manager, the overview section can sum up the total managerial experience of fifteen years. That keeps a resume reader from overlooking or having to study the resume to discover that information.

The Purpose of the Overview

This section offers a summary of the important points in the resume and draws conclusions about the candidate's work experience that would otherwise take a lot of time for the resume reader to dig out. The overview collects and summarizes your abilities and skills. Some accomplishments are pointed out in this area when they relate specifically to the job for which the resume was created. This summary saves the resume reader time by adding up years of experience accumulated while at several companies. The proof of all the claims made in the overview must be contained in the work history. The overview also keeps an employer from missing information contained in the work history that takes a little more careful reading to dig out. A good overview will match the list of criteria an employer has and sometimes match part of the interview questions about key skills.

What Belongs in an Overview

- Show your strengths and key accomplishments.
- List areas of expertise when applicable to the job.
- Include marketing abilities, entrepreneurial skills, management skills, and interpersonal skills.
- Sometimes include statements about important work ethics such as stating *self motivated*, or *can work independently*.

Certain personality traits may be mentioned:

Example

- An aggressive, focused operations professional with a demonstrated ability to build teams and accomplish goals.
- Proven ability with implementing cultural and technological change in difficult environments, producing positive results.

You may mention certain skills that give you an edge for this job:

Example

- Fluent in Spanish and French.
- Extensive worldwide travel and global business relationships throughout Europe.

This area can resemble a list of qualifications:

Example

- Proven track record of developing new business while expanding current account base.
- Ability to establish rapport with prospects and clients.
- Quick and thorough when learning new product lines.

Work history can be summarized:

Example

- Over twenty-five years of experience as a plant manager.

Or:

- Senior financial executive with experience in the publishing, advertising, printing and consumer products industries.
- Skilled in controls, SEC reporting and compliance, treasury, tax, merger acquisitions, and depositions.
- Accustomed to multi-location and international operations.

This is a great place to include special training that is pertinent to this job:

Example

- Have ISO9000 certification.
- Experienced in union negotiations.

What Doesn't Belong in an Overview

Certain information is better presented in a cover letter. That information includes:

- Any work situation on the resume that may be viewed in a negative light. Maybe after a month at a new job you were fired or quit. Always keep any such explanations neutral. Say something like the culture wasn't a good fit. Don't say that they deceived you about the job, and you left. Never say anything critical or negative about a previous employer.
- Information that may explain lapses in employment of more than one year.
- Irregularities in the work experience (such as dual jobs) that may need a little more explanation.
- Leave out hobbies, general interests, personal information, and any claims not supported by the work history in resume and cover letters.

Overview Don'ts

- Don't put too much in an overview. A good resume is no more than two pages and you are never allowed to make the font extremely small to include excess information. An overview should seldom be more than one third of a page and can be less. Get to the point and make that point worthwhile.
- Don't make long, single-word lists of talents. Employers will skip these unsupported words. Single-word lists waste precious resume space.
- Don't gripe about anything.
- Don't put information that sheds a negative light on you.
- Don't use statements that are too brief and/or too broad.
- Don't state objectives. Most employers can guess you are interested in a job at their company and the position they have opened by the fact that you sent them a resume.
- Don't repeat the same point in a slightly different way. Say it clearly and actively once only.
- Remember, the overview is a brief summary. Don't go into great details about your skills and abilities. That belongs in an interview.

Cover Letter Information

Some of the information that doesn't belong on a resume may belong in a cover letter. Please consult a book that specializes in creating cover letters. However, if for some reason using a cover letter is not possible, and you feel you need to use part of the overview to explain certain issues, do so sparingly.

Constructing the Overview

- Make the sentences or sentence fragments strong, active, to the point, and easy to understand.
- Make sure claims made in the overview are supported in the work history.
- Use bulleted lists to summarize the highlights of the resume. This is the preferred way to present the information. Sometimes a short paragraph may be used in place of a bulleted list. If you use a paragraph, make it no more than three to five lines in length, or about a quarter of a page.
- Tailor each sentence or sentence fragment to best explain the quality you want to highlight.
- Remember that the two things that affect the overview most are the work history and the needs of the employer.
- It is okay to abbreviate something when you are positive the resume reader will know its meaning.
- Sum up total years of experience that may be spread over several jobs when that experience relates to the job for which you are applying.
- This is the area to point out working traits that are strategic. For example: Readily accepts responsibilities. Always sees job through until done.
- Draw attention to activities that support your work status in this field.
- Point out key skills the employer is looking for.

- This may be a good place to mention if you are willing to travel. That information may have an impact on the employer's perception of your ability to perform the job you are seeking.

Modify the Overview For Different Resumes

The overview area may change for different jobs. It isn't unusual for salespeople to have a lot of sales and marketing experience. If you are applying for a marketing position, emphasize marketing experience in the overview. If you are applying for a sales position, show sales data.

When You Don't Need an Overview

Sometimes you are sending out a generic resume to many potential employers and you can't tailor your overview adequately. Although for some resumes, an overview gives a resume a competitive edge, sometimes a resume is perfectly acceptable and effective without one.

- If you have a lot of information that you need to retain in the work history section, and even after editing, you feel the work history can't be reduced to two pages, leave off the overview and leave in the work history.
- If your work history doesn't group well into overview information, leave off the overview.
- It is better to have no overview than to have a poorly constructed one.

Make Sure Your Overview and Work History Agree

The overview can state that you can and have painted the moon, but if there is no evidence in the work history to support this claim, the statement comes across as a gross exaggeration or bald-faced lie. Be sure that statements made in the overview are supported by the work history. Be sure that you summarize the important work history in the overview. Remember, the overview is your chance to offer employers something they can quickly refer back to that tells them why you are a strong candidate.

Chapter 4

Fonts and Formatting

Fonts and Formatting—The Professional Touch That Puts You Above the Competition

When only a few resumes are submitted for review, employers are more willing to wade through poorer quality resumes. No matter how many resumes are submitted, a resume that looks professionally prepared stands out in the pile and invites an employer to read it. Neatness, appropriate use of white space, and a readable font size all contribute to professional appeal. The poor fax-ability of small fonts has already been emphasized, but fonts that are too small have an additional consequence. When there are a lot of resumes to review, it is only natural for the resume reader to start skimming parts of the resume. Small fonts that are densely packed can receive an inadequate reading that leaves important information overlooked.

Good formatting of a resume that includes a good font choice and strategic use of white space sends a subliminal message of professionalism. No matter what job is applied for from a construction worker to a company president, a neat and professional resume shows a potential employee in a positive light. In addition, a resume with good eye appeal has a better chance of being selected to be read before the resume reader is exhausted. Lastly, a correctly prepared resume will survive the fifteen-second read.

Resumes People Like to Read

The winning resume style presented in this book has a professional look, in part through formatting and font choice. At a glance, the resume looks professional and easy to read. This presentation allows the resume to come across a fax machine legibly, even when the resume is faxed several times. Similar information is easily recognized and the spacing gives groups of information a logical order. This chapter gives a step-by-step procedure on how to format the raw material so that you can achieve the same professional look as the resumes used throughout this book. The formatting techniques in this chapter allow you to create a finished product that invites the reviewer to read it. Problems such as needing to fit a little more on a page without looking crowded and using less material without looking sparse are addressed in Chapter 8.

More Advantages of Formatting:

Often when sending your resume to different potential employers, small modifications are needed to highlight skills certain employers need to know about. Formatting a resume simplifies customizing each resume submission. The time spent with the initial formatting saves time later when reconstructing the final look, especially if last minute changes are needed. Without formatting, each time you tweak the resume before submission to a different employer, you may spend hours redoing tabs and spaces. These can suddenly take on the appearance of a train wreck when one or two additional words are added. You can avoid that train wreck altogether by using formatting from the beginning. Instead of spending hours on tweaking your resume for a specific employer, you will only spend minutes.

Formatting prevents certain errors. Inconsistent spacing jumps out at some people, but not others. You may not catch spacing inconsistencies, but the resume reader might. Whether conscious or unconscious, inconsistent spacing sends the wrong message.

Using a proper format means the final piece comes across a fax machine with all the contents easily readable.

A proper format makes it easy for the resume reader to get a quick feel for what you have to offer.

Fonts

Font Choices and White Space

There has been a scientific study of the choice and use of fonts and the strategic use of white space. For this book, a professional in page layout determined the best font and the best use of white space. For your resume, two of the best fonts to use for legibility are Book Antiqua and Bookman Old Style. Book Antiqua is preferred. The best size to use with these two fonts is twelve points. The section *The Science of Fonts* explains why these are good choices.

Some Popular Choices of Fonts

Perhaps the most popular font used is Times New Roman. Other popular fonts are Courier New and Arial. Book Antiqua and Bookman Old Style have significant advantages over Times New Roman, Courier New, and Arial. For those who need an explanation as to why their favorite font is a poorer choice, read the next section. If you must use Times New Roman, you need to make 13 points the minimum size or you can run into legibility problems after the resume is faxed.

The Science of Fonts

Few people realize the extreme technology and programming that went into creating fonts for a computer. There is a big difference between creating a resume on a typewriter and creating one with a word processor, even when you use a font similar to a typewriter font (the Courier fonts). To create fonts for word processing on a computer, someone sat down and decided how wide and tall each letter would appear. Then they decided just how close together letters could be and how much space to put between letters and words. For most fonts, typing a period at the end of a sentence means that all you need to do is put one space afterwards, and the word processor will make that space the correct distance. If you type two spaces, you've added too much space.

Another area where font programmers have already dealt with the correct spacing is dashes. Dashes have three lengths; the word processor adds enough space before and after each dash so you don't have to add any. If you add a space, readers will strain their eyes more and the information will appear detached.

Another area in which fonts vary is with the space between lines in a paragraph. This results in some font choices that read well in books not working as well for a resume.

Font Measurements

Fonts are measured in points units and spaces are measured in pica units. There are 54 points to a pica. The 54 points was the width of the letter m plus its space. That is where the term *em dash* and *en dash* comes from. You will use em dashes and en dashes when you create your resume. A hyphen is the width of a standard space in the font. Just as each font varies in height of letters and spacing between letters, the width of the hyphen varies. The minus in true typesetting is a width different from the dash. At one time, numbers were shorter than the upper case letters. Nowadays, numbers are as tall as upper case letters and the minus sign is about the same length as the hyphen. Spacing between words and lines in Book Antiqua and Bookman Old Style is greater than in Times New Roman. This makes Book Antiqua and Bookman Old Style easier to read. This is why they are preferred for resume use.

Variable Spaced Fonts

There are two types of variable spaced fonts. In the first type, the "x" is taller than it is in the second type. The width of the x affects readability because a greater height in the "x" makes the letters in the words appear closer together than the short height does. The width of the m's is another factor. The wider "m" and a shorter "x" aids older eyes that strain more readily when reading. People over forty who have diminished reading ability make a lot of the top hiring decisions.

Some fonts that are good for books aren't good for resumes or letters. In part that is because books have adjusted the leading. The leading is the space between the lines. If you choose a font that is hard to read, the appeal of your resume is reduced and it may end up in the reject pile. All of this can create a headache for resume writers when seeking that professional appearance for their resume. Fortunately, a highly-skilled former typesetter, who now does word processing and layout on computers, and who has strong computer-formatting skills, has worked all this out for the readers of this book.

If you've learned little else from this discussion of fonts, remember: The programming for fonts is extremely complicated. A lot of the fonts have already been programmed for the correct spacing after periods and the different kind of dashes. If you add an extra space before and/or after the dash, you create a poorer product.

Analysis of Some of the More Popular Fonts:

Courier looks like someone sat down at a typewriter and picked away at the resume. On page 61 is an illustration of different fonts. Courier is included in the examples. Courier is what is known as a mono-spaced font. Perhaps the way to best describe a mono-spaced font is to imagine a row of identical sized boxes lined up one after the other. Inside each identical box is a letter. The largest letter inside the box is the m which stretches from one side of the box to the other. The i is centered inside the box. mmmmmm   iiiiii. Notice that six i's take up as much space as six m's. With mono-spaced fonts, most letters are almost identical in size and appear evenly spaced.

The other kind of font is called a variable-spaced font. Again picture those rows of boxes. For a variable-spaced font, the box sizes are all different. The letter i has a smaller sized box than the letter m as seen in the following example using Times New Roman: iiiiii mmmmmm. Notice six i's take up less room than six m's in a variable spaced font.

All characters in a mono-spaced font are the same width. At a glance, this kind of type pales when compared to many of the darker, sharper looking fonts available with word processors. Another problem that can exist with mono-spaced type is the distance between certain letters, such as I and l, are almost as far apart as if they were in separate words.

Times New Roman

Times New Roman is a popular proportionally-spaced font. The examples on page 61 show the same resume using Times New Roman. With proportionally-spaced fonts, the spacing between letters in each word varies, and the spacing between words is almost even. For resumes, Times New Roman isn't the best choice. The spacing between each letter is very narrow. When you use a 12-point font in Times New Roman, the original copy isn't as easy to read as Book Antiqua or Bookman Old Style using a 12-point font. Once a resume using Times New Roman is faxed, the first faxed copy becomes harder to read than the original, and the second time it is faxed, many words become harder to decipher. Part of the solution is to use a 13-point font as the minimum size for Times New Roman. This size difference still doesn't read as well compared to Book Antiqua or Bookman Old Style after several times through a fax machine.

> With most fax machines, the first time you fax a copy of a resume, the fax reduces the quality of the original copy by 1% to 2%. Each time a resume is re-faxed, its quality is further reduced.

Arial

Arial is shown in the examples on page 61. Arial is less friendly for readability on a resume, because the font isn't a Serif font. Serifs are little lines used to finish off the main strokes of the letters, such as those found at the tops and bottoms of the letter m. Serif fonts are easier to read because they have little hooks on them that hold the eye on the line.

When faxed, Arial font does okay, but after the resume is transmitted a couple of times, the lower case "a" and "e" fill in and the numbers are not as clearly discernable.

Book Antiqua and Bookman Old Style

Book Antiqua and Bookman Old Style are the top choices for resumes. Book Antiqua and Bookman Old Style are shown in the examples below. The preferred font size is 12 points. Book Antiqua is better but it is not offered on all computer programs. Book Antiqua does a good job of maintaining legibility after repeated faxing. Unlike Times New Roman, there is no need to adjust the spacing between lines and paragraphs to maintain legibility.

An Illustration of Different Fonts

Below are examples of different fonts using the same 12-point size while typing the same sentence. Look at the x's at the end of each sentence. You can get a good idea about the font height and spacing looking at these two x's. Note that with Arial, the x's look attached at the bottom.

Examples

Mono-Spaced Font

Courier New:

```
The family of white rabbits jumped into the garden extra high
without any cares in the world. Which is real neat. (Xx)
```

Proportionally-Spaced Fonts

Times New Roman:

The family of white rabbits jumped into the garden extra high without any cares in the world. Which is real neat. (Xx)

Arial:

The family of white rabbits jumped into the garden extra high without any cares in the world. Which is real neat. (Xx)

Book Antiqua:

The family of white rabbits jumped into the garden extra high without any cares in the world. Which is real neat. (Xx)

Bookman Old Style:

The family of white rabbits jumped into the garden extra high without any cares in the world. Which is real neat. (Xx)

The spacing between the lines varies because the spacing between the lines is programmed into the word processing program. As a result, with Arial the y and h almost touch between the two lines.

Look at the letters m, h and w in all the fonts. Notice the difference in the widths. The narrow appearance of these letters in Times New Roman inhibits readability.

Although all of the examples are the same size, 12 points, Courier takes up too much room as compared to Book Antiqua. Courier is designed to imitate typewriter print. Book Antiqua and Bookman have the advantage that they take up less room than courier and still maintain legibility when faxed. And they are easy for most people to read. Times New Roman takes up the least amount of room at 12 points, but does so by making some letters narrow and most letters closer together at the cost of ease in readability. This readability suffers more after transmittance over a fax machine. The smallest font size needs to be 13 points, and 14 is better if you use Times New Roman. This takes away all the advantage of the smaller size, and doesn't resolve the loss of readability caused by the closer spacing of the letters. Most people find Times New Roman very taxing to read for long periods of time.

Formatting

Computer Criteria

This chapter will tell how to format a resume in Microsoft Word using Windows Millennium or Windows 98. The examples were created using Microsoft Word 95 and 97. These procedures were later tested using Windows 95 and minor variations were observed. The screens you see on your computer may vary slightly from those shown here, but you should have no trouble understanding how to perform these procedures.

Using the Menu and Tool Bar

Below is an illustration of the Menu and Tool bar available in Microsoft Word.

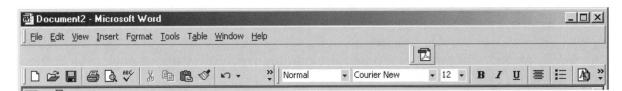

On the Tool bar above, the word Normal indicates what kind of style is currently applied to the document. The box next to that which states Courier New tells the font type. The next box tells the font size. If the Style and Font box isn't on your Tool bar, you can add it by selecting *Tools>Customize>Toolbars*.

Using an Old Resume

You can use an old resume if you remove the formatting, and then transfer the typed text. Inside a new document where you insert the old resume, you can create your style sheet. Follow these steps if you are using an existing resume.

1. Open the old resume.
2. Change your normal style font to Book Antiqua (or the font of your choice).

3. Highlight the old resume and apply the new Normal font, changing the entire contents of the resume to an unformatted Book Antiqua.
4. Copy the converted resume into a new document.
5. Save the new document with a new name for the resume.
6. Now you are ready to create a style sheet for the resume. The style sheet will allow you to tag the text, resulting in a professionally formatted resume.

Step 1 and 2: Open the Resume and Change the Font

Open your old resume.
From the Menu bar, select *Format>Style*.
From the *Style* box, select **Normal**.
Click on the *Modify* box. From the *Modify Style* menu, select *Format>Font*.
The *Font* box appears. Select **Book Antiqua** (if that is your font of choice). Note that **Book Antiqua** is not available on some versions of Microsoft Word. **Bookman Old Style** is similar to **Book Antiqua**.
From the *Font Size* box, select **12** for 12 points.

The Font box should appear like the one shown below. Be sure your font of choice (such as **Book Antiqua**) is selected under *Font*, that **Regular** is chosen for *Font Style*, and the *Size* is **12**. If the font box shows these choices, click OK. This will return you to the previous screen. Keep clicking OK until you reach the last screen. Then click Apply.

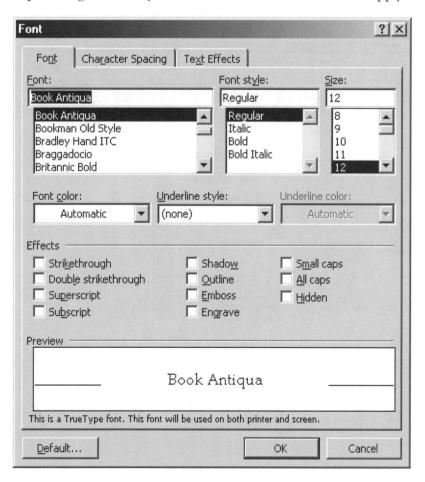

Step 3: Apply the New Normal Font

The *Normal* font needs to be applied to the entire text in your old resume. To do this, from the Menu bar, choose *Edit>Select All*. Your drop down menu may be different from the one shown here, but it will have the *Select All* option.

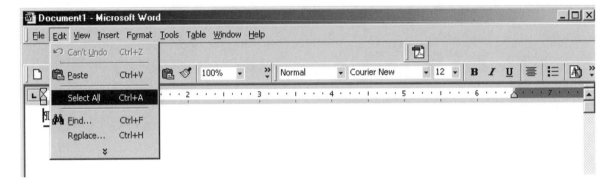

You will see your old resume highlighted in black.

Click on the down arrow beside the *Normal* tag field on the Tool bar. A drop down menu similar to the one below will appear. Select the Normal tag and click on it. This will change the entire document to Book Antiqua.

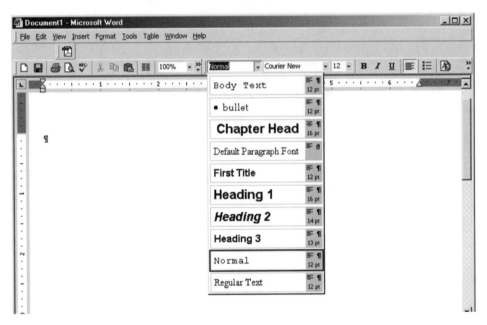

Step 4, 5 and 6: Copy Into a New Document and Save

From the Menu bar, choose the *Edit>Select All* command to highlight the entire document. Choose *Edit>Copy*. Choose *File>New>Blank Document*. Choose *Edit>Paste*. This transfers your resume into a new document. Choose *File>Save as...* and enter a new name for your new file.

Step 6 is Detailed below under *Creating a Style Sheet*

Creating a Style Sheet

Creating a *style sheet* allows you to make a consistent *tag* for each category of information on the resume. For instance, all of the company names can have a consistent appearance because you *tag* them with identical formatting commands. Initially, setting up tags takes a little time, but later time is saved when you make changes to your resume and you don't have to keep readjusting the information to make sure each area is consistent in presentation. You can create a style in a new document, or in an old resume that has been stripped of formatting.

Tags

The following tags are recommended for use in your *style sheet*:
Name
Address
Heading
Company
Job Title
Bullet (Used for the bulleted information found in the job history.)
Normal (Used for typing in basic information prior to formatting or tagging.)

See page 66 to view an illustration of these tags in the *Basic Template for a Resume*

Basic Template/Style Sheet for a Resume

NAME

Address
City, State Zip
Phone
Email
(The Address tag includes all the contact information above.)

HEADING: (Used for Overview, Professional Experience, and other categories.)

- Type overview information here. Use the bullet on the Tool bar.

PROFESSIONAL EXPERIENCE: (Use the Heading tag.)

Company — City, State (The entire line is tagged for Company.)   *Date*

* *Job Title (the tag style is called Job Title)*

General information in a paragraph form (**use Normal style on the Tool bar for the tag**).
- Bulleted information. (Use the bullet contained under Styles found on the *Tool* bar.)

Company — City, State   *Date*

* *Job Title*

General information in a paragraph form.
- Bulleted information.

EDUCATION: (Use the Heading tag.)

This area contains your college education. This part is in `Normal` style.

SPECIAL TRAINING OR SKILLS: (Use the Heading tag.)

This area contains information presented in **Normal** style.

Setting Your Style's Normal Font

The *Normal* style is applied to text by highlighting the text and then selecting the **Normal** style from the *Tool* bar. This is illustrated on page 64. To set your *Normal* style for your document, from the *Menu* bar select *Format>Style*.

The following box appears:

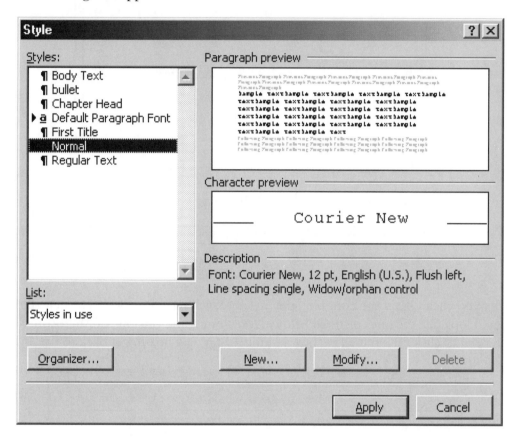

The *Style* box shows that the settings for the *Normal* style are Courier, 12 pt. These settings need to be changed to your font choice for your resume. For the following examples, Book Antiqua, 12 points is used as an illustration.

To change your *Normal* style to *Book Antiqua*, select *Modify* from the *Style* box viewed above. This will display the font box (seen on page 68). Scroll through your font selections until you find Book Antiqua. After you change the setting to *Font*: **Book Antiqua**, *Font style*: **Regular**, *Size*: **12** (as shown in the font box on page 68), click OK.

Note: For some versions of Microsoft Word, *Modify Style* dialog box comes up. That's where you choose *Modify>Font* to get the *Font* box.

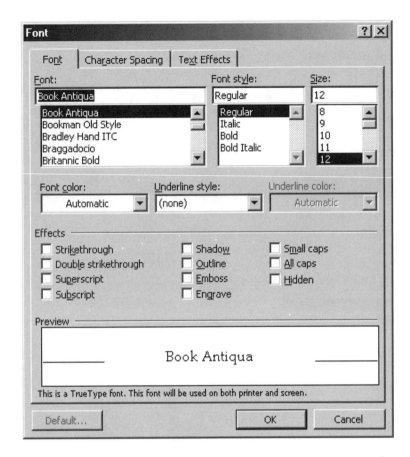

After you click OK in the Font box, the Style box will return to view. The new settings should look like the ones pictured below. *Note:* For some versions of Microsoft Word, you will need to click OK in the *Font* box and the *Modify Style* box to get back to the *Style* box.

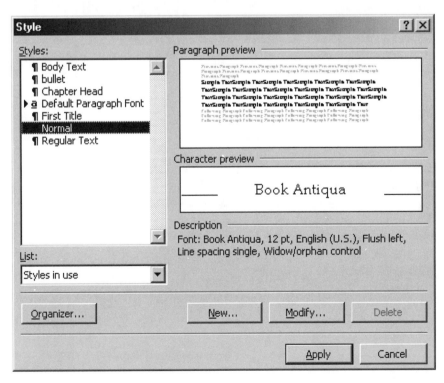

Creating Your Tags

Tags allow you to command your typing in a document to conform to a preset formatting style. To create a *tag*, first name the tag. Then set parameters for the *font*, *paragraph* and any *tab* settings. Each tag will have its own style setting.

To name and set the parameters for a *new* tag, from the Tool bar, select *Format>Style*. The following box appears:

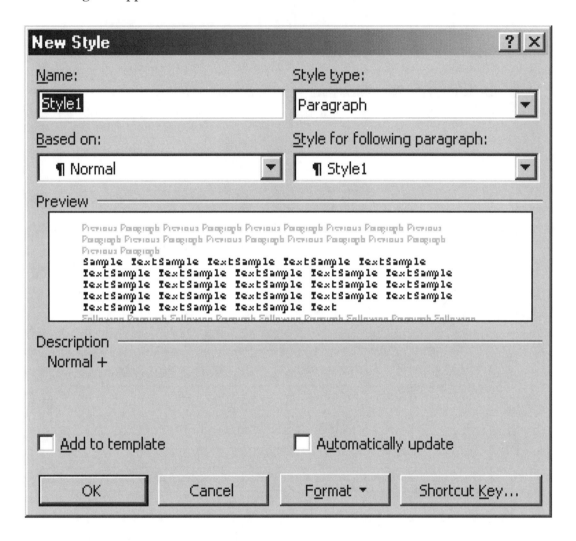

Choose a name for the tag you are creating and type it in place of the word *Style1*. For this example, the tag *Company* will be created. To get started, type the name *Company* in place of the word *Style1*.

Note: For some versions of Microsoft Word, Select *Format>Style* and the Style box appears. Then choose *New* in the *Style* box to get the New Style box

Setting the *Font* for a Tag

From the *New Style* box, select *Format*. From the popup menu, select *Font*. The following box will appear:

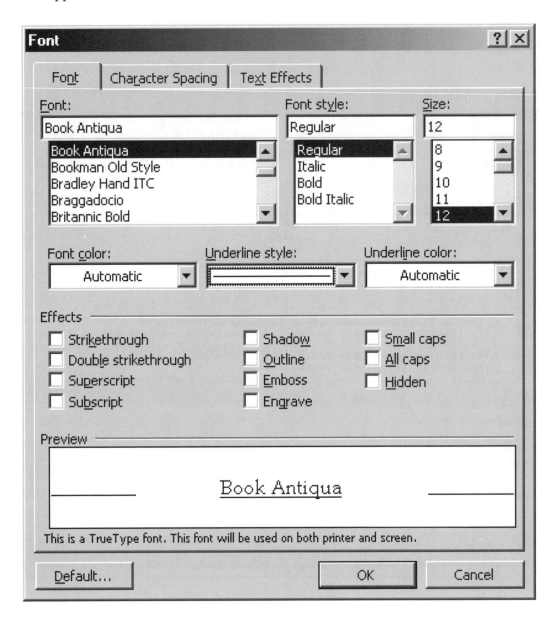

In this Font box, you can set parameters for your font type, style and size; underling; and effects. For the *Company* tag, make sure the settings are *Font*: **Book Antiqua**, *Font style*: **Regular**, *Size*: **12** as shown in the box above, and that the regular *Underline style* is set to display what is seen above. Then click OK.

Setting the *Paragraph* for a Tag

From the *New Style* box, click on *Format>Paragraph*. The following box will appear:

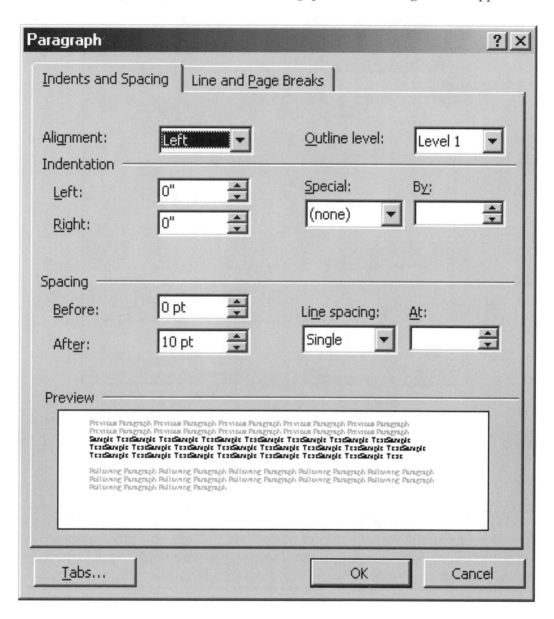

In this box you can set *Alignment, Indentation, Hanging* indents, and the *Spacing Before* and *After* the paragraph. For the *Company* tag, change the *Spacing* setting for the *After* box to **10 pt**. Then click OK.

Setting the *Tab* for a Tag

From the *New Style* box, select *Format>Tabs*. The following box will appear:

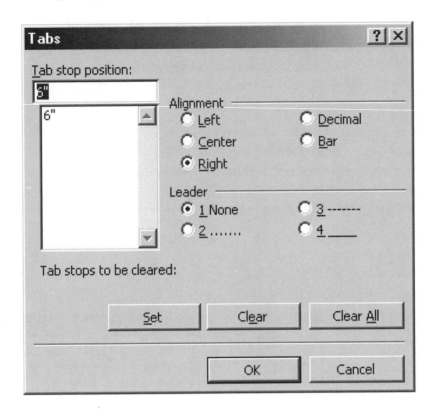

If there are any tabs showing in the box, highlight them and click on *Clear*. After the tabs are cleared, set the tab for *Company*. To set the *Company* tab, set the *tab* for **6"** and then click OK. The 6" tab should be all that is displayed when you close the box.

You will find formatting easier if you have the paragraph mark appear on your screen. The paragraph mark is added by clicking that icon on the Tool bar. You may have to look for the paragraph mark under the additional Tool bar items located under the >> symbol with a down arrow underneath.

Soft Returns

If you have a second line for company information, you will need to enter a soft return. To enter a soft return, hold down the *shift* key when you enter a *return*. On the computer screen, the soft return will look like a bent arrow at the end of the line instead of the normal paragraph return that is shown for a hard return. Failing to enter a soft return will result in too much spacing added between the first and second line for the company information or for the address and contact information.

Using Your New Tag

You can now tag all your company information. Simply type in the information that belongs on the line, or highlight information brought in from a previous resume. Now click on the word **Company** from the *Style* box on the Tool bar as illustrated below.

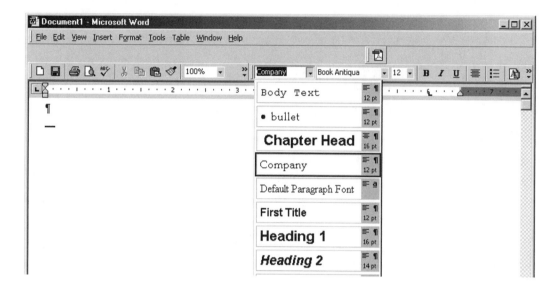

When you click on the company box (highlighted in the dropdown menu above) this is what your text should change to:

Company — City, State   *Date Started–Present*

To get rid of the extra underlined area, use you mouse to highlight that area, and then click on *U* from the Tool bar. Or you can access underline from the menu: *Format>Font>Underline* and then click on none.

Your final product should look like:

Company — City, State   *Date Started–Present*

Other Formatting Issues With The Company Line

Adding a Second Line
If you need to add a second line of information to the company line, be sure to use a soft return (Shift + Return). Page 72 tells more about soft returns.

Using the Correct Kind of Dash
The dash used after the company name is called an *em dash*. This dash is longer than the one found on the typing keyboard. The dash used between the dates is also a longer dash and is called an *en dash*. The information on page 74 tells you how to create these dashes.

> ### "Em" Dash and "En" Dash
> The regular dash on the keyboard is meant for usage between hyphenated words. A longer dash is used to represent pauses or interruptions in the reading material. An "En" dash is used between dates.
>
> Regular dash: A ten-gallon bucket.
>
> To insert a long dash or "Em" dash, while holding down the Alt key and the Ctrl key use the dash from the numeric key pad on the far right. Notice how much longer the em dash is compared to the regular dash above.
>
> The Smith Company—A Fortune 500 Company
>
> To insert a medium size dash or an "En" dash, hold down the Ctrl key and use the dash from the numeric keypad on the far right. The en dash is a little shorter than the em dash, but still longer than a regular dash.
>
> Worked 1996–Present
>
> *Do no put spaces before or after the regular, em, or en dashes. The word processing program already put in the correct amount of space.*

Formatting the Rest of Your Tags

The *Name, Address, Headings,* and *Job Title* tags formatted parameters can be created using the general guidelines given for the company formatting tag. Simply substitute the desired tag's name and use the specific formatting style listed below.

Name

Naming the Tag
Format>Style>New
Type in under the *Name* box the word **Name**.

Font Setting
Format>Font
Book Antiqua, *Font Style:* **Bold,** *Size:* **14**
Find *Effects* and click the box for **All caps** (a check mark will appear).

Paragraph Setting
Format>Paragraph
Alignment is changed to **Centered**
Find *Spacing* and enter **10** pt in the *After* box.

Address

Naming the Tag
Format>Style>New
Type in under the *Name* box the word **Address**.

Font Setting
Format>Font
Book Antiqua, *Font Style*: **Bold**, *Size*: **12**

Paragraph Setting
Format>Paragraph
Alignment is changed to **Centered**
Find *Spacing* and enter **22** pt in the *After box*.

> A hard return, or regular return will result in 22 points of spacing to appear behind the end of each line. To keep the address and phone numbers from being spaced so far apart, use a soft return after the end of each of these lines. Only use the hard or normal return at the end of the final line. The soft return is explained on page 72.

Headings

Headings include Overview, Professional Experience, Education, Special Skills and other main areas of organization.

Naming the Tag
Format>Style>New
Type in under the *Name* box the word **Heading**.

Font Setting
Format>Font
Book Antiqua, *Font Style*: **Bold**, *Size*: **12**
In the *Effects* area click on **All caps**.
Find *Underline style* and click for a *regular underline* (the single line).

Paragraph Setting
Format>Paragraph
Find *Spacing* and enter **10** points in the *After:* box.

Job Title

Naming the Tag
Format>Style>New
Type in under the *Name* box the word **Job Title**.

Font Setting
Format>Font
Book Antiqua, *Font Style*: **Bold Ital**, *Size*: **12**.

Paragraph Setting
Format>Paragraph
Find *Spacing* and enter **10** points in the *After:* box.

Tab Setting
Format>Tabs
Set the tab for **0.2** inches.

Using the Job Title Tag

Practice using this tag by opening a blank document. Then type an asterisk, enter a tab, and type in your job title. Then enter a return. The line should look like this:

```
*       Job Title
```

After you apply the tag, the finished product will look like this:

* *Job Title*

A Microsoft Word Formatting Error Seen With Job Title
Note: When typing an * followed by a tab, then using the return, Microsoft Word changes the star into a dot. To correct this: Edit/Undo AutoFormat.

If you see a bullet suddenly appear in place of your asterisk after you use a return, you need to use Undo AutoFormat.

Bullets

There are two kinds of bullets. The first, the bullet under the Overview has no indent for the bullet. The second, the bullet used under the Work History for accomplishments, has an indent.

Bullet for the Overview

Type the word Bullet inside an open document. Then enter a return.

Highlight the word *Bullet*. On the Tool bar, click on the *Bullet Icon*. The default setting should give you a result that looks like this:

Example

- Bullet

If the bullet is any other shape or color, modify as follows:
From the *Menu* bar, under *Format>Paragraph,* check that the setting for *Special* is **Hanging**, and that the setting for *By:* is **0.25"**.
From the Menu bar, under *Format>Bullets and Numbering:*
Click on the correct *bullet box.*
Select *Customize.*
Set the following:
Bullet Position: Indent <u>a</u>t: **0"**
Text position: <u>I</u>ndent at: **0.25**
Now click OK

Bullets For The Work History
Naming the Tag
Format>Style>New
Type in under the *Name* box the words **Bulleted Work History**, click OK.

Font Setting
Format>Font
Book Antiqua, *Font Size*: **12**.

Paragraph Setting
Format>Paragraph
In the *Indent Left*, type in 0.25".
Click the down arrow for the *Special* box. Select Hanging from the drop-down menu.
In the *By* box right next to it, type in **0.25"**.

Tab Setting
Format>Tabs
Set the *Tab* for **0.5"**.

Selecting the Bullet
Format>Numbering
Click on Format/Numbering
Select the correct bullet.
Then click OK.

Your final product should look like the example below once your formatting has been applied:

Example

- Bulleted Work History Accomplishments

The difference between the two bullets is the amount of indentation from the left margin. An example of the differences in how the bullets appear can be seen on page 66, *Basic Template/Style Sheet for a Resume*.

Bullet Dilemmas

Sometimes after you set your *bullet* for accomplishments for the work history, the bullet on the Tool bar changes its settings. To correct this, go back through the directions and reset to the correct settings for an Overview bullet.

Spacing After Periods and Other Entries

When using word processing programs on computers, the correct spacing is coded in for periods, slashes, semicolons, colons, zip codes, initials, and before and after dashes. You only need to add one space before or after any of those items. If you do add two spaces, the final product will have too much space. The exception is when you are using a Courier font which imitates a typewriter.

Page Layout

Adding a Header on Top of the Second Page.

The second page needs a header that tells your name and the page number. To do this, first change the page layout so the header only prints on the second page.

Changing the Page Layout
File>Page Setup
Choose the *Layout* tab and under *Headers and footers,* click the box for **Different First Page**.

Adding the Header
From the Menu bar, select *View>Header and Footer*
While your curser is in the *Header* box, type in your header information. Put in your name, add a tab, then type the word *Page*. Now highlight the entire line.
From the Menu bar select *Format>Tabs*
Set the *tab* for **6"**.
From the Menu bar select *Format>Font*
Set the *font* for **Book Antiqua**, **Bold**, **Italic**.
From the *Header and Footer popup* Menu bar, click on the # at the end of the six inch tab. The # will enter the correct page number on the page. (Use the first #, the one that doesn't have a hand.)

Saving as a New Document

When you modify your resume for different jobs, be sure to save each modified version under a new name. To do this, click on *File>Save* As. Now enter a new name that helps distinguish this version from other functional versions.

Common Formatting Problems to Avoid

A resume with formatting problems sends unwanted messages. Some of the common problems include:

- Tiny type for the address and phone number that is located off in a corner. That important information can't be read from a faxed copy.
- An obscure format for the company names where you worked.
- Job titles hard to locate, making it difficult to associate similarities in work experience and consistencies in the work history.
- Poor page breaks that leave the name of the company you worked for on one page and the information that belongs underneath on a separate page.
- Insignificant information underlined while the important information is obscure.
- A different pattern of presentation for the information that belongs together. This inhibits someone from doing a quick read-through. For instance, some resumes have different font types or sizes for the company and the date, making this information which needs associated appear to be disconnected.
- Too much space between information that belongs together, and not enough space between information that should be more separated gives a chaotic appearance. Several things can cause spacing problems. Paragraph marks can vary in the amount of space they represent, and some have extra space programmed in under the Format>Paragraph>Spacing command. These can disrupt the continuity when skim reading information.

Sometimes these resumes are discarded altogether. Other times they are put on the bottom of the review pile, allowing a candidate with less qualifications a better opportunity for the job.

Chapter 5

A Look At Resumes That Failed

Some Bad Resumes Will Slip By

Good and bad resumes are sent to employers every day. Sometimes poor resumes actually land someone an interview for a job. This can happen when an employer has few resumes to review, or few viable candidates to interview. Because a resume is often the first contact you have with an employer, the more positive and professional your resume is, the better first impression you will make. Likewise, poorly presented resumes sometimes send subliminal messages that steer an employer away from a candidate even before they meet face to face.

What Makes a Resume Work

Resumes that work all have the following characteristics:

- Pertinent skills are usually summarized in an overview.
- Job titles are easy to locate and read.
- At a glance, an employer can see a candidate's jobs and how long the candidate worked at each different job.
- The job history is presented in an easy-to-skim-read format. In today's economic climate, job history is the real selling point for a person. In the job history, an employer can assess what the person did at each job, see the accomplishments, and view how long the person worked at various companies. Sometimes a job description is included. Accomplishments follow in bulleted form. The sentences are power-packed and to the point. Typically, the stronger the work history in a field, the greater the candidate's appeal. Similar job skills need to be easy to identify at a glance.
- Education is shown briefly but completely. Other applicable skills, professional affiliations, and any awards are listed under separate headings.
- Overall, the finished product is neat and professional in appearance. The resume is well-organized and its contents are legible after faxing or emailing.

The Power of the First Page

Although one- and two-page resumes are quickly becoming the standard, in some ways all resumes are one-pagers. This is true because the first page is in view more often than the second page. A poor first page may stop an employer from reading on, so whenever possible, make sure the best information about your work history appears on the first page of your resume. For example, if a short-term job can be moved to the second page without disrupting chronological order, do so. If a job that helps to emphasize your credentials can appear on the first page with a little reformatting, make that extra effort. How to better arrange resume information is in Chapter 8.

Although the perfect resume doesn't exist, the better the work history, the closer the candidate may come in meeting the employer's requirements. The following rules give guidelines for creating effective resumes and the illustrations show pitfalls to avoid.

Rule 1

Make a Good First Impression with a Professional Format.

Take a look at the Lori Rook resume on page 81. This resume didn't even receive a fifteen-second read. It went straight into the trash can. It was later dug out to be used as an example.

The resume was tossed because the stair-stepping design came across as unprofessional and the faxed copy was almost illegible. The font is Times New Roman and the size is 8 point. As far as the content, the summary of qualifications only scratches the surface of what Lori may have to offer. The statement "fifteen years of combined work experience" doesn't really say what kind of work experience. The statement "responsible for generating several long-term account relationships" needs more explanation, and needs some examples and support in the work history.

The work history is little more than a company name and title. No accomplishments are shown. The education information is fine, but hard to read. The Hobbies section and the Interest and Activities section are a complete waste of space and reading time. The objective is actually counterproductive because it states too many diverse goals. Diverse goals don't give an employer the impression that a person is committed to one job position. In the end, there isn't enough information here to reformat into a suitable resume or to interest an employer.

Lori Rook
P.O. Box 20
Eagle, NM 87719
(505) 388-4256

Summary of Qualifications
With fifteen years of combined work
Experience, I have acquired multiple skills
as an account representative. I have been
responsible for generating several long-term
account relationships. The service of these
accounts included a full spectrum of customer
support beginning with the original sale to the
final completion of the print project.

Education
1979 - 1984
Western Washington University
Bellingham, WA
BA in Graphic Design with a
focus on Printing Technology
BA in Art Education K-12

Professional Experience
1992 - 2000
Allied Printers
Seattle, WA
Account Representative

1991 – 1992
Graphics Inc.
Kirkland, WA
Account Representative

1985 – 1991
Smith Lithographic
Seattle, WA
Account Representative

1984 – 1985
Canyon Printing
Lynnwood, WA
Manager

Objective
I would like the opportunity
to expand and diversify with
a company that is challenging and
progressive in all levels of art,
sales, customer support
and production.

Hobbies
Watercolor painting,
camping, hiking,
gardening, travel and
Native American Studies.

Interest & Activities
Currently involved in several different community projects for
environmental awareness such as
Pes Patch gardening program
Heirloom Seeds and ancestral
planting methods

Rule 2

Don't Send a Negative Message with a Poor Formatting Style.

Some of what a resume communicates is subliminal. A lot of employers have little trouble throwing out a resume with a lot of typos and grammatical errors, writing the person off as sloppy. Although a resume with a poor formatting style including poor font choices is often read, it can send unwanted messages. For example, some fonts are difficult to read, and you don't want your reader to have a hard time reading your resume. If a format is cluttered and packed, the material can cause a reader to feel tense. You don't want that negative image associated with your name. The end result can be an employer reading your resume and concluding, "I can't put my finger on it, but I just didn't get a good feeling from reading the resume."

Take a look at the Ruth Shield resume on page 84 and see what kind of message the format and font tells us. Do you get the impression from this resume layout that Ruth will take charge and get a job done? Or do you perceive Ruth as someone who stays in a corner, out of sight and hopes no one bothers her with any questions?

An Analysis of Ruth Shield's Resume

The left and right margins on this resume are 1.25 inches and 0.81 inch respectively. This makes the text out of balance with the page. (Already this candidate is perceived as a little "off balance.") To check this "look" on your resume, use Print Preview in Word to get an idea of the balance and aesthetic appeal.

The top margin is 0.56 inch, and the bottom margin is 0.88 inch. The small top margin starting so close to the top will probably cause her name to be cut off when the resume is faxed. Even if the resume is hand-delivered or sent by regular mail, companies often distribute copies internally for further evaluation, and they often use a fax machine to do this. With the name cut off after faxing, more work is created for office people. That doesn't make a good impression.

The font size is also a problem. Not only is it too small to fax properly, it is hard to read on the original. If other resumes sent in have more appealing fonts, they will probably be read first, or more thoroughly. If you choose to use Times New Roman, use 13 point. Squeezing down to 12 point is pushing the far limits and causes a loss in readability after the resume is faxed several times. Using a font as small as 10 point is asking to lose out to the competition before the first word is read. On Ruth's resume, there was plenty of room to use a larger font, because the resume only spans one and a half pages.

Helping to diminish the readability of this particular resume is the full justification. Full justification belongs in newspapers and magazines, but not on resumes. When it is used in newspapers and magazines, the lines of type are often adjusted to avoid some of the more difficult spacing, which is an artifact of this kind of justification. Few people using it for resumes make those adjustments. For resumes, left justification is the preferred method.

The spacing of paragraphs on this resume doesn't allow for easy skimming, nor does it do anything for eye appeal, nor does it emphasize important points. The job descriptions and accomplishments presented in paragraph form are a disadvantage. This kind of information is dry by nature; its presentation in a paragraph makes reading even more tedious.

The resume is shown reformatted on page 86.

Take a look at some of the changes. The overview is bulleted to make it easier to read. The sentence "Strong analytical skills." was added. Ruth knew her analytical skills were a strong part of her appeal, which is why she put it first on the original resume. Since it is more traditionally located on page two, the statement in the overview helps bring immediate attention to this valuable asset.

Rearrangement For Success

Ruth attempted to increase the organization of the technical skills by using italics on the original resume. See how much more efficient the redone version is by using boldface along with the italics. Not all information needs this kind of emphasis, but for Ruth's field, the technical skills are very important and warrant the extra attention.

The dates are changed from month and year to show only the year. This makes that very pertinent information easier to grasp at a glance.

The final reformatted resume was tweaked to fit on two pages. More about how to do this on a resume is in Chapter 8.

Will Ruth's original resume actually have a negative effect on employers? Ruth had presented her resume to many companies with no positive response. After the material was reorganized and reformatted, Ruth had three job interviews within one week and accepted one of the job offers. She got the job because she had the talent, but to get the job, she needed an interview. Her original resume wasn't getting her those interviews.

Ruth Shield
16645 Child La.
Cheyenne, WY 82001
(307) 243-2134

Overview:

Eighteen years of experience spanning all phases of the system development life cycle; Analysis, Design, Coding, Testing, Implementation, User Training and Documentation. Business experience in telecommunications, publishing, inventory, purchasing, marketing, directory and real estate applications.

Technical Skills:

Programming Languages: Informix-4GL, Informix-SQL, FOCUS, SQL, COBOL, VSAM, QMF, FILEAID, REXX, EXEC

Databases: Informix, DB2, FOCUS, Stratagem

Editors: VI, ISPF, XEDIT

PC Software Applications: MS Word, MS Excel

Operating Systems: Unix (DG, Sun), MVS, TSO, VM, Windows, DOS

Training/Education:

Jan. 2000 – Took an Oracle class.

1980 – B.S. Management Information Science, University of Cheyenne, Cheyenne, Wyoming

1978 – A.A. Liberal Arts with emphasis in Mathematics, Cheyenne Community College, Cheyenne, Wyoming

Job Experience:

Computer Solutions (Landis & Co) – Consultant (08/1998 – Present)

    KOB (11/1998 – 12/1999) – Performed a Y2K impact analysis on Informix Code for an undocumented system. Later, analyzed and documented an undocumented Informix database. Exported pertinent data using Informix-4GL and UNIX shells from the old UNIX/Informix platform to a AS400/DB2 platform.

    Morgan (Cheyenne) (08/1998 – 10/1998) -- Coded and tested enhancements for Y2K interface for time entry applications. The system ran on a UNIX platform with Informix code and database. UNIX shell scripts were used to import data. Pvcs was used to maintain software changes.

    Code and tested a new system to create internal electronic messages/broadcasts to employees. This included a message maintenance area, reading the messages and an auto-delete facility. The system ran on a UNIX platform with Informix code and database. Shell scripts were used to run the auto-delete portion.

Basic Communications – Programmer/Analyst (12/1995 – 08/1998)

    Analyzed and coded a business system that was online, menu driven for the business areas of Inventory Control, Purchasing. Provided user support for the areas plus order entry and customer information. Worked on two upgrades of vendor software of Endura (Fourgen) software. The system ran on a UNIX platform with Case tools, Informix code and database.

ATT Communications – Programmer/Analyst (02/1982 – 11/1995)

Worked as an assistant Programmer/Analyst and was then promoted to a Project lead. Provided all aspects of the development and enhancement phases over the time. This application was both online and batch, importing data from an outside system. The system ran on an IBM 3090 mainframe platform with MVS, TSO, COBOL, FOCUS with a DB2 interface. JCL with FILEAID, JES3, CA7 was used to run the application at night.

Designed and successfully implemented a system where the current information was separated from the history in different databases. The result was to reduce the response time by more than half, yet maintain a consistent flow of the current system. The system ran on an IBM 3090 mainframe platform with MVS, TSO, COBOL, FOCUS with a DB2 interface. XPEDITER was occasionally used for debugging purposes. JCL with FILEAID, JES3, CA7 was used to run the application at night.

Designed and implemented a system for a marketing group that was online. The system ran on a MVS platform, with CSP and DB2.

Designed and coded numerous data conversion programs. Platforms included, MVS, VM, Honeywell. Languages included COBOL, VSAM, EZTRIEVE, FOCUS, REXX, EXEC, FILEAID. Databases included DB2, IMS, FOCUS.

Picked up a barely started development of a marketing query system written in a 5th generation language, INTELLECT. The system utilized DB2 databases.

Maintained and enhanced a vendor system which ran on a MVS platform using STRATAGEM for its database and language.

Coded and tested a system which was converting a directory system with advertising from a MVS platform with COBOL and IMS to a Honeywell system.

Maintained and enhanced a system on a Honeywell system written in COBOL and FORTRAN utilizing an IDS-II database.

Ruth Shield

16645 Child Lane
Cheyenne, Wyoming 82001
Home: (307) 243-2134

OVERVIEW:

- Eighteen years of experience spanning all phases of the system development life cycle, including analysis, design, coding, testing, implementation, user training, and documentation.
- Business experience in telecommunications, publishing, inventory, purchasing, marketing, directory, and real-estate applications.
- Strong analytical skills.

PROFESSIONAL EXPERIENCE:

Computer Solutions (Landis & Co) — Based in Denver, CO   *1998–Present*

* *Consultant, KOB Project, Topeka, KS (1998–2002)*

- Performed a Y2K impact analysis on Informix Code for an undocumented system.
- Exported pertinent data using Informix-4GL and UNIX shells from the old UNIX/Informix platform to an AS400/DB2 platform.
- Analyzed and documented Informix database.

* *Consultant, Morgan Project, Cheyenne, WY (1998)*

- Coded and tested enhancements for Y2K interface for time-entry applications with a system that ran on a UNIX platform with Informix code and database. Used UNIX shell scripts to import data and PVCS to maintain software changes.
- Coded and tested a new system to create internal electronic messages broadcasted to employees. Included message maintenance reading, and an auto-delete facility. The system ran on a UNIX platform with Informix code and database. Shell scripts were used to run the auto-delete portion.

Basic Communications — Cheyenne, WY   *(1995–1998)*

* *Programmer/Analyst*

- Analyzed and coded an online, menu-driven business system for inventory control and purchasing.
- Completed two upgrades of the vendor software Endura (Fourgen). The system ran on a UNIX platform with case tools, Informix code and database.
- Provided user support, order entry, and customer information.

Ruth Shield   *Page 2*

<u>*ATT Communications—Provo, Utah*</u>   <u>*(1982–1995)*</u>

* *Programmer/Analyst (1986–1995)*

Technical project lead for a sales and compensation application.
- Developed and enhanced online and batch applications including importing data from an outside system. The system ran on an IBM 3090 mainframe platform with MVS, TSO, COBOL, and FOCUS with a DB2 interface. JCL with FILEAID, JES3, and CA7 was used to run the application at night.
- Designed and implemented a system to separate current information from history in databases and reduce response time by more than half while maintaining a consistent flow of the current system. The system ran on an IBM 3090 mainframe platform with MVS, TSO, COBOL, and FOCUS with a DB2 interface. XPEDITER was occasionally used for debugging purposes. JCL with FILEAID, JES3, and CA7 was used to run the application at night.
- Designed and implemented an online system that ran on a MVS platform, with CSP and DB2 for a marketing group.
- Designed and coded numerous data conversion programs. Platforms included, MVS, VM, and Honeywell. Languages included COBOL, VSAM, EZTRIEVE, FOCUS, REXX, EXEC, and FILEAID. Databases included DB2, IMS, and FOCUS.
- Independently took a fifth generation language (Intellect) project from the start, and with no guidance, produced the end product the company needed.
- Maintained and enhanced a vendor system which ran on a MVS platform using STRATAGEM for its database and language.
- Coded and tested a system which converted a directory system with advertising from a MVS platform with COBOL and IMS to a Honeywell system.
- Maintained and enhanced a system on a Honeywell system written in COBOL and FORTRAN utilizing an IDS-II database.

* *Assistant Programmer/Analyst (1982–1986)*

TECHNICAL SKILLS:

Programming Languages: Informix-4GL, Informix-SQL, FOCUS, SQL, COBOL, VSAM, QMF, FILEAID, REXX, and EXEC
Databases: Informix, DB2, FOCUS, Stratagem
Editors: VI, ISPF, and XEDIT
PC Software Applications: Microsoft Word, Microsoft Excel
Operating Systems: UNIX (DG, Sun), MVS, TSO, VM, Windows, and DOS

EDUCATION:

BS, Management Information Science, University of Wyoming, Cheyenne, WY, 1980.
AA, Liberal Arts with emphasis in Mathematics, Community College, Cheyenne, WY, 1978.

TRAINING:

Oracle class, Jan. 2000

Rule 3

Never Ask an Employer to Play the "Match Game."

Take a look at the Harold Grant resume on page 89. This resume is what is called a "Play the Match Game" resume. If employers have time, they can match up the relevant experience with the job listed in the employment section. Harold made some of the matches a little easier by stating a company on a few of the lines where he lists his experience. Matching up experience with employment history takes a lot of time. Some of the accomplishments can't be accurately matched without speaking to the candidate who owns the resume. Never expect an employer to spend the time and resources to figure out the valuable information that should appear immediately after the job title.

Style Issues

The main problem with this style is that the experience section prevents the resume reviewer from relating progress and accomplishment at each position worked. There is no sense of how much time Harold spent making these accomplishments.

Formatting improvement needed with Harold's resume includes a change in font. The resume is currently in Times New Roman with a font size that varies from 10 point for the text to 14 point for the headings. As mentioned previously, 10 point is too small for easy reading and for readability after faxing. Harold only used a page and a half for the entire resume. He could easily have made the font larger and easier to read on the original.

The Objective is counterproductive. Potential employees sound more reliable if they state only one interest (the one for the job they are sending this resume in for) rather than a selection of job interests. An employer wants to feel as if Harold has a specific interest in his particular job, not just any job. Stating two interests in an objective doesn't give that impression.

The employment section has inconsistencies in the style of presenting the state. Initials represent most of the states, but one is spelled out. The states need to be spelled out or abbreviated, but not mixed. The comma after each job title needs to be edited out. The information about the jobs is crowded and hard to pick out from the company title. It is better to put the city and state on the same line as the company, and not on the line with the division title. Often division titles can be left off altogether. There is an alignment error for the company in Rochester, New York introduced by the use of tabs. For *Containers of America, New York City* is an incorrect reference. The city of New York is stated as New York and never as New York City.

Howard needs to give more information about his patents. What are they for and when did he receive them? The awards also need elaboration. The Miscellaneous category has some initials that an employer may not recognize, which makes the information useless. The education category does little to let us know what kind of education Harold actually has. He did something when he attended the University of Iowa, but what and when isn't apparent. The same is true with Dupont College. The statements *Supervisory Management*, *Business Management*, and *Paper and Pulp Technology* may be classes, courses, or seminars. On this resume those words lose their significance because the information is not clear.

Harold Grant
201 First Street
Greenwood, IN 46143
317-888-2370

Objective

To secure responsible position, using my management and creative experience in **structural design** and **mechanical packaging** or **sales**.

Employment

Manager, Packaging Design and Mechanical Packaging Rainbow Industries, Carton Division	1/97 to Current Greenwood, IN
Senior Packaging Engineer, Mechanical Packaging, Structural Design Midwest Packaging Corp.	5/93 to 1/97 Dayton, OH
Director and Manager, Packaging Design and Mechanical Packaging Douglas Packaging, Inc.	3/86 to 5/93 Harrison, Ohio
Manager, Packaging Design Falcon Packaging	3/81 to 3/86 Rochester, NY
Manager, Packaging Design Containers of America	9/70 to 3/81 New York City, NY

Experience

- Created structural designs, using paperboard, plastics and various materials.
- Duplicated and improved customer packaging to create a product that ran within companies manufacturing specifications.
- Developed and implemented Structural Design Department while employed with Douglas Packaging sending carton sales from $40 million in 1986 to $110 million in 1992.
- Directed, supervised and scheduled structural packaging designs.
- As Senior Packaging Engineer, from 1993 to 1997, supported the sales group by responding to customer complaints. Assisted customers with acquiring new machinery or modifying present machinery.
- Created new structural designs and modified current designs, making them more compatible with the customer's equipment.
- Coordinated carton and machinery projects with customers, suppliers, production personnel, salesmen and carton design staff.
- Worked with customers in the music, cosmetic, entertainment, pharmaceutical, tobacco, food, batteries, toys and retail fields.
- Made packaging designs and machinery proposals presentations to customers.
- Trained staff members to make samples of structural designs and become designers.
- Create designs using CAD/CAM system.
- Worked directly with customers, buyers, packaging engineers and production managers.

Awards and Patents

- 20 US and foreign patents
- Many packaging awards from Paperboard Packaging Council (PPC)
- Numerous awards from the National Paperbox Association (NPA)

Miscellaneous

- Served on advisory board of National Paperbox Association (Package Design Council)
- Keep current with new machinery by attending PMMI and CMM Machinery shows and exhibits.
- U.S. Air Force: honorable discharge.

Education

Supervisory Management
Business Management
Paper and Pulp Technology
Williams University of Iowa
University of Iowa
Dupont College, Williams, IL

Rule 4

Put your best foot forward.

Look at the Sam Parker resume on page 94.

Sam's resume style is out-of-date. Over twenty years ago the rule of thumb was to put education first. In today's competitive job market, anyone with a sound work history needs to put that work history first. Work history almost always supersedes education and is what will appeal to an employer the most. For employers, the best resumes have *both* strong work experience and solid education in the field. Next in rank are resumes with strong work experience. Next are those that show education in the field. Even with jobs in cutting-edge fields, in which new technology is emphasized, relevant work history takes precedence over education because it indicates your ability to apply what you've learned in your work environment. Most employers know to look for a Skills section in your resume to see if you offer the right technical skills. Stating the work history first is how you put your best foot forward by showing an employer how your used those skills.

Job Organization and Presentation

In general, Sam's entire resume is in need of reorganization and rewriting. Sam has a lot of work experience in the field of Production Manager (a field that he is trying to re-enter), so he should emphasize his work experience in that area. The way to emphasize important work experience on this resume is to be brief on the details of more recent jobs. Those jobs are in a subordinate field so Sam needs to emphasize his history from a few years ago when he was working as a Production Manager.

Sam needs to address why he isn't working as a Production Manager. This is done best in a cover letter. In addition, Sam can strengthen his experience as a Production Manager by stating it in the first bulleted item in the overview. The rest of the overview needs to concentrate on supporting his Production Manager skills, not his other skills.

Page 96 shows the redone resume.

Better Font Choices

The font choices in this resume were the first to be revised.

At first glance, this tiny 8-point Arial font is unappealing to read for a full resume. The script-like font used for Sam's name is Bush Script, 14 point. After only one faxing, this imitation handwriting style of font appears shaky. That's not something Sam wants to project to an employer.

After changing Sam's resume to a better font such as Book Antiqua, 12 point, the original resume spanned three pages. This is too long for a resume (two pages is the ideal target, one page is also acceptable). Some people try to squeeze their resume into two pages by using a smaller font. What they really need to do is edit their resume. Just because you provide lots of information for an employer, doesn't mean the employer will actually read it. The excess information wastes an employer's time and often results in the employer not concentrating on your impressive qualifications.

The education section now appears at the end and it is given a better presentation.

Better Work Experience Presentation

Several problems in the work experience needed to be fixed. The two most recent positions, Technical Support Agent and Failure Analysis Technician, are jobs of less prestige and responsibility than the position of Production Manager. In the first two job descriptions, the amount of information needs to be reduced. This is true especially for the second job where Sam worked less than a year. The only reason to emphasize either of these jobs would be if Sam were applying to a company that worked with similar products or technology. This isn't true in the present case. As a general rule, something needs to be mentioned about jobs in similar fields, but jobs in dissimilar fields need no description of job duties. If Sam took a job as a framer on a construction crew for a few months in between jobs in his field, he doesn't need any detail of what he did at that job. Sam needs to de-emphasize his less important jobs by reducing or eliminating the job duties and accomplishments.

Editing Out Insignificant Work Experience

In Sam's work experience, some of his older work history needs to be deleted. Sam did his cooperative education more than ten years ago. In comparison to his postgraduate experience, the pre-graduate experience has diminished in value and can be completely removed. Cooperative education offers students a taste of work in their field. With no other work experience, and only education, cooperative education gives the graduate an edge. However, when there is postgraduate work experience available, the cooperative education quickly looses its value and just takes up valuable space on the resume.

What needs to be preserved in Sam's work history are the things Sam accomplished in his different jobs. Because Sam is interested in again obtaining a Production Manager position, he needs to emphasize his work experience in that position on his resume. His current resume shows his work experience at every job he has held. All jobs are treated as equally important when they are not.

Eliminating Useless Statements

Statements that need to be left out on any resume are ones like "Promoted to Product Marketing Manager from Product Manager Assistant." That fact is apparent when one looks at the job title changes and dates.

Handling Acronyms

Throughout Sam's work history, abbreviations and acronyms appear that may have significance to Sam and his coworkers at a particular job, but don't convey any information to a potential employer. These items need to be eliminated and replaced by information that has more significance. Sam also has capitalized some words inappropriately. He probably did it for emphasis, but such techniques are annoying to employers.

Organizing Special Training into Categories

Another problem with Sam's resume is that he has dispersed his specialized training classes in his work experience. Training and technical skills belong in their own sections, not mixed in with work history. Employers want that kind of information available at a glance. Some employers will search for a technical skills heading on a resume. If they don't find that information, very often the resume isn't read.

A Final Tightening

After trimming down unnecessary work history and cleaning up unnecessary capitalization and acronyms, the work experience was reworded to tighten and eliminate unnecessary information.

After the makeover, Sam's revised resume has less information about his jobs, but what is there is extremely significant. Don't make the false assumption that putting more in a resume means that all you present will be read. Quite often the opposite happens. Instead of slogging through unnecessary or poorly presented information, many resume readers will just not read any of it and move on to read a better one.

Samuel R. Parker
4520 Smith Road Seattle, WA 98101
(206) 348-2041

Education
⇒BACHELOR OF SCIENCE IN ELECTRICAL ENGINEERING⇐
Concentration in VLSI design and semiconductor device physics
University of Montana, Helena, Montana, August 1989

Work Experience
⇒ TECHNICAL SUPPORT AGENT ⇐
Techtronics NetServer Group
Techtronics, Seattle, WA; October 2001 to Present

- Provide on-line support to Techtronic's US-based Net Server customers. Trouble shoot customer hardware and software related problems and dispatch Customer Engineers with replacement parts. Serve as an online resource for pre-sales questions and assist with post-sales NetServer upgrades.
- Completed five week training course covering:
  - Techtronics NetServer System Architectures including the 8-Xeon processor LH4.
  - Intelligent I/O technology including SCSI RAID.
  - Network Operating Systems including Windows NT Server, Novell Netware, Lxoix and SCL UNIX.
  - Networking hardware and software protocols including TCP/IP.

⇒ FAILURE ANALYSIS TECHNICIAN⇐
Motorola/Lucent Products
Lutina Technologies, Palo Alto, CA July 1998 to October 2001

- Responsible for PCA product quality throughout the shop and first line troubleshooting support for functional test and automated test including: reducing process defects to improve first pass test yields, analyzing/repairing ICT functional failures and performing root cause analysis. Responsible for Shop Floor Data Management process flow and documentation.
- Major Accomplishments:
  - Worked with Motorola/ Lutina Engineering Team to manufacture ITR-Class-3 Tritium Satellite PCBs.
  - Utilized Techtronic 2300-1 to diagnose/repair Motorola/ Lutina PCBs.
  - Diagnosed & repaired Techtronic Visualized system boards.
  - Trained/Certified for SMT Extra-Fine Pitch Sodering/Rework, IPC-610B PCA Quality Standards, and ESD Class Manufacturing.

⇒PRODUCTION MANAGER⇐
Westside Products
Motorola Inc., Fort Worth, TX October 1997 to October 1998

- Responsible for PCA product quality throughout the shop and first line troubleshooting support for functional testing.
- Managed Product Development for the 1490's Westside Wonder Product Line. Including the 1493 and 1494 Physical-Cable Interface, AOOC/AIIP Native Bridge and PCI Bridge Standard Products.
- Responsibility included implementing Product Release Process, creating Project Management schedules and managing Cross-Functional team effort to meet scheduled product release dates.
- Major Accomplishments:
  - Served as Project Manager for diverse-site Engineering team consisting of R&D, Product, Test and Quality Engineering to insure all necessary functional and product quality tests were performed in order to meet formal Product Release-to-Manufacturing criteria and schedules.
  - Created/Maintained Intranet Website for the communication of Project Management schedules & activities.
  - Promoted Motorola Logic's 1490"s Product Line at week-long Comdex Convention hosted in Las Vegas for an estimated 250,000 international participants.
  - Successfully negotiated partnership with Compaq Computer for their procurement of Westside 1492 PHY
  - Completed knowledge of Hewlett Packard technical training course.

⇒PRODUCT MANAGER⇐
Confrontational Scopes, Helena, Montana July 1995 to October 1997

- Managed cross-functional team consisting of Development Engineering, Process Engineering, Product/Test Engineering and Order Management in order to meet the needs of specific ASIC customer accounts including AG Communications, Executioner Electronics, Techtronics and Tranwitch.

- Responsible for quoting new ASIC products, managing ASIC product flow from development through release and managing existing ASIC customers' product quality and delivery issues.
- Major Accomplishments:
    - ➢ Successfully managed the transfer of all customers' ASIC products resulting from the plant closure in Wyoming and moving to Montana including all appropriate qualifications needed in order for these customers to seamlessly adopt their new product.
    - ➢ Created, organized and executed most successful product promotion in company's history.
    - ➢ Promoted to Product Marketing Manager from Product Manager Assistant

⇒PRODUCT MANAGER ASSISTANT⇐
Confrontational Scopes, Helena, Montana July 1991 to October 1995

- Researched and analyzed and wrote ASIC product marketing study.
- Researched and analyzed High-Speed Analog Fiber Optics Market, including large customer survey resulting in the definition of new High-Speed Tran impedance Amplifier.
    - ➢ Created technical literature, completive analysis, marketing strategies, press releases, sales training, advertising and pricing for over forty High-Speed Amplifier products that generated $11.5million.
    - ➢ Presented New Product Training & Competitive Analysis presentations at Corporate Annual Sales Meeting consisting of independent representative sales force.

⇒INSTRUCTOR⇐
September 1990 to May 1991

- Created and instructed a new computer programming course focusing on Java programming language requirements of Sophomore Electrical & Computer Engineering students.

⇒CO-OPERATIVE EDUCATION STUDENT⇐
TOP Microelectronics
May 1988 to September 1988

- ASIC Cell Development Group
    - ➢ Assisted lead engineer in the development of new and the enchantment of existing 1.5mm and 2.0mm CHOS library cells.
    - ➢ Performed electrical characterization using SPICEUP to create CAD timing data for design tools.
    - ➢ Crated physical cell databases and performed layout extraction to determine parasitic parameters.

    May 1987 to September 1987
    - ➢ Wrote C program to generate scalable RAM & ROM netlists to be used in customer's new ASIC designs.
    - ➢ Semi-Custom Design Group
    - ➢ Assisted lead engineer with the full characterization of TOP's new 1.5mm cell library.
    - ➢ Calculated ASIC cell timing data drawn from water probe test data.

Samuel R. Parker

4520 Smith Road
Seattle, WA 98101
Home: (206) 348-2041

OVERVIEW:

- Experienced Production Manager.
- Skilled at taking a product line from development through promotion.
- Strong communication skills including the use of intranet Web site.

PROFESSIONAL EXPERIENCE:

Techtronics, NetServer Group—Seattle, WA   *2001 to Present*

* *Technical Support Agent*

Provide on-line support to Techtronic's US-based Net Server customers, including troubleshooting hardware and software-related problems.

Lutina Technologies—Palo Alto, CA   *1998–2001*

* *Motorola/Lucent Products Failure Analysis Technician*

Responsible for product quality throughout the shop and first-line troubleshooting.

Motorola Inc.—Fort Worth, TX   *1997 to 1998*

* *Production Manager*

Responsible for PCA product quality throughout the shop and first-line troubleshooting support for functional testing.

- Managed development, and then implemented product release, including project management schedules and cross-functional team effort for the 1490's Westside Wonder product line. Insured all necessary functional and product quality tests were performed to meet formal product release-to-manufacturing criteria and schedules. This product line included a physical-cable interface and standard bridging products.
- Promoted 1490's product line at weeklong Comdex Convention hosted in Las Vegas for an estimated 250,000 international participants.
- Created/maintained intranet Web site for improved communication.
- Successfully negotiated partnership with Compaq Computer for their procurement of Westside 1492 PHY.

<u>*Confrontational Scopes — Helena, MO*</u>   <u>*1991 to 1997*</u>

* *Product Manager (1995 to 1997)*

Managed cross-functional team consisting of Development Engineering, Process Engineering, Product/Test Engineering and Order Management departments in order to meet the needs of ASIC customer accounts. Responsible for quoting new ASIC products, managing ASIC product flow from development through release, and managing existing ASIC customers' product quality and delivery issues.

- Successfully managed transfer of all customers' products during the plant closure and move.
- Created, organized, and executed most successful product promotion in company's history.

* *Product Manager Assistant (1991 to 1995)*

- Researched and wrote ASIC product marketing study.
- Research of high-speed analog fiber optics market resulted in the definition of new High-Speed Tran-Impedance Amplifier.
- Created technical literature, competitive analysis, marketing strategies, press releases, sales training, advertising, and pricing for over 40 high-speed amplifier products that generated $11.5 million.

<u>*University of Wyoming — Cheyenne, WY*</u>   <u>*1990 to 1991*</u>

* *Instructor*

SPECIAL TRAINING:

Techtronics NetServer System Architectures including the 8-Xeon processor LH4.
Intelligent I/O technology including SCSI RAID, 2001.
Network Operating Systems including Windows NT Server, Novell Netware, Lxoix and SCL UNIX, 2000.
Networking hardware and software protocols including TCP/IP, 1999.
Trained/Certified for SMT Extra-Fine Pitch Soldering/Rework, IPC-610B PCA Quality Standards, and ESD Class Manufacturing, 1998.

EDUCATION:

BS, Electrical Engineering, Concentration in VLSI design and Semiconductor Device Physics, University of Montana, Helena, Montana, 1989

Rule 5

Don't Leave Off Important Identification Information.

Take a look at the Carol Holland Resume on page 100.

In the heading, Carol needs to identify what kind of telephone number she has given. Is this her home, work, or a cell phone? The periods between the numbers are not as good as parentheses or dashes for people trying to read and dial a phone. Also, if she has an email address at which she can safely receive correspondence, she should list it. With an email address, you don't need to identify it as such. Anyone who knows how to use an email program can figure out from the @ what the address is. The ZIP code is also needed on her address.

Overall Resume Improvements

- When Carol used Times New Roman, she used a 12 point font. It would have been better to use a minimum of 13 point to help ensure the integrity after repeated faxing.
- The word *resume* is never necessary on a resume.
- In her address, the abbreviation for Illinois is either IL with no periods or Il. IL is the preferred abbreviation.
- The career summary is acceptable, but Carol needs to have someone else read over her work. People always have a hard time catching their own errors. Carol has a few errors in tense that detract from her professionalism. Carol also has a date error. She states she worked for Newport from October 1992 to Present, but she states her first job as a Purchasing Trainee starting in July of 1987.
- At first glance, the presentation of the different positions may come across as work at different companies. She needs to indent or somehow make the work positions subordinated to the main company statement. Although she uses italics bold for the job position and regular bold for the company, the final product doesn't readily distinguish the two items.
- Carol has spacing errors when using dashes, and she uses those spaces with her dashes inconsistently. Employers may well hope she isn't as inconsistent in her work.
- Her work history is justified. This adds a challenge for readers. Most of the wording needs to be tightened and reworked. Either paragraphs or bulleted lists present the information adequately and effectively.
- In the work history, Carol tells us whom she reports too in her current job. Leave that kind of information out. It adds no significance outside of your circle of coworkers and only wastes space on a resume.
- The second page header needs her name instead of the word resume. That way if the second page gets shuffled in with someone else's material, it can easily be put back with her first page.
- The Interests section needs to be cut. It adds no value to her as a potential candidate.

The Revised Resume

Page 102 shows the resume improved.

With her resume reformatted, it is easier to see that Carol was employed at one company, and while there, she worked her way up from Purchasing Trainee to Production Purchasing Manager. Only presenting one company on a resume is fine in Carol's case because this was the only job she worked at in her field after she graduated from college. Additional work history adds no value.

Taking out the month for the employment dates makes it easier to quickly determine how long Carol was at each position.

Resume

Carol L. Holland
201 Topper Lane
Chicago, I.L.
309.591.2214

CAREER SUMMARY

More than seven years production experience at one of the largest direct mail company in the United States. Expertise includes strong knowledge of inline press equipment, lettershop processing, and understanding of marketing driven workflow. Exposure to large spectrum of successful direct mail campaigns, ranging from promotional to fulfillment related efforts.

EXPERIENCE

Newport Publishers Chicago, IL – Purchasing Division   October 1992-Present

Manager – Production Purchasing   **March 2000 - Present**
Currently responsible for managing day-to-day production of targeted and repeat-order direct mail campaigns as well as the Acknowledgement and Billing Program (including fulfillment/renewals), amounting to a budget of well over $20 Million dollars annually. Report directly to Vice President of Production/Purchasing and supervise seven direct reports in the group. Prepare mailing budgets, cost analysis, production schedules, and hold meetings as needed. Perform employee evaluations and reviews as scheduled for the staff.

Senior Purchasing Agent   **February 1997- March 2000**
Assisted the Assistant Director of Technical Development with new format test inline packages. Used knowledge of inline packages. Used knowledge of inline press to achieve significant cost savings on rollout packages. For example, researched tested format with vendors and helped discover that with slight modifications in size, the format could yield much higher production rates when produced on a inline imaging press. As a result, production on redesigned format increased 50%, costly were lowered dramatically, saving approximately $250,000.00 on first rollout of the package.

Purchasing Agent   **August 1993 –February 1997**
Supervised Purchasing Trainee to purchase Billing and Renewal mailing. Worked closely with Marketing on package development of specialty products such as metal and foil coins, magnets, and detailed 4-color brochures. When package was produced on an uncommon expensive stock, proposed changing substrates to less costly laid stock. Consequently, PCH maintained package look while decreasing costs $30,000.00 for the campaign.

Junior Purchasing Agent   **June 1992- August 1993**
Exposure to many large volume mailings requiring planning and monitoring of production to meet in-home mailing schedules. Worked closely with fulfillment Marketing and Creative to

reduce high production costs. In order to maintain the package design on a weekly-used envelope, suggested to Marketing and creative to reprint a label on stock instead of affixing label, which proved costly. This change contributed a $200,000.00 annual saving- the program continued for approximately five years, compiling a $1,000,000.00 cost savings.

Purchasing Trainee   **July 1987 –June 1992**
Introduced to direct mail production, which included the Billing and Renewal efforts. After six months, given full responsibility for these programs attending production meetings, soliciting vendors bids for mailing. Visited printing plants for tours and press oks. Attended several print seminars and workshops to develop 4-colour prepress and printing knowledge.

EDUCATION
Chicago University, Chicago, IL   1983-1986 Bachelor of Business Administration, Major in Marketing

COMPUTER SKILLS
Strong knowledge of most commonly used business computer software such as Microsoft Word, Microsoft Excel and Quark Express.

INTERESTS
Lead a Girl Scout Troop of twelve girls

Carol L. Holland

201 Topper Lane
Chicago, Illinois 60610
Home: (309) 591-2214
Carol@aol.conm

OVERVIEW:

- More than seven years production experience at one of the largest direct mail companies in the United States.
- Strong knowledge of inline press equipment, letter shop processing, and understanding of marketing driven workflow.
- Exposure to large spectrum of successful direct mail campaigns, ranging from promotional to fulfillment related efforts.

PROFESSIONAL EXPERIENCE:

Newport Publishers/Purchasing Division — Chicago, IL　　　　　　*1987–Present*

* *Production Purchasing Manager (2000–Present)*

- Responsible for managing day-to-day production of targeted and repeat-order direct mail campaigns as well as the Acknowledgement and Billing Program (including fulfillment/renewals), amounting to a budget of well over $20M annually.
- Supervise seven direct reports in the group. Prepare mailing budgets, cost analysis, production schedules, and arrange meetings.
- Perform employee evaluations and reviews.

* *Senior Purchasing Agent (1997–2000)*

- Assisted with new format test inline packages.
- Used knowledge of inline press to achieve significant cost savings on rollout packages including a project that increased production on redesigned format 50% and reduced cost $250K on first rollout of the package.

* *Purchasing Agent (1993–1997)*

- Supervised Billing and Renewal mailing.
- Worked with marketing on package development of specialty products including metal and foil coins, magnets, and detailed 4-color brochures.

- When package was produced on an uncommon expensive stock, proposed changing substrates to less costly laid stock. Consequently, PCH maintained package look while decreasing costs $30K and maintaining quality appearance.

* *Junior Purchasing Agent (1992–1993)*

- Large volume mailings requiring planning and monitoring of production to meet in-home mailing schedules.
- Worked with fulfillment Marketing and Creative to reduce high production costs.
- Saved $200K annually over a five-year period with reprint of label on stock material, replacing the use of an affixing label.

* *Purchasing Trainee (1987–1992)*

EDUCATION:

BA, Marketing, Chicago University, Chicago, IL, 1986

COMPUTER SKILLS:

Strong knowledge of Microsoft Word, Microsoft Excel and Quark Express

Rule 6

Avoid One-Liners.

Look at the David Heel resume on page 105.

Overall this resume is better than most that are received. Although three different fonts are used on the resume, they are used effectively. This is something few people can do this well. Either David has studied in this field or has a natural talent. Most of the tabbing used during formatting and regular spacing came through fairly intact when the piece was emailed.

The two parts of the resume that need the most improvement are the Professional Profile and the Experience sections. The work history needs to be written more powerfully and inappropriate capitalization needs to be removed. Also, personal pronouns need to be eliminated from resumes.

The Professional Profile wastes space with the statement "I'm seeking a challenging position in which I can use my management, experience, and communication skills to help an organization grow." That point needs to be left to be discovered in an interview.

The Experience section wastes space because it is presented in a one-liner format. These single words really don't tell an employer anything significant. For instance, take the word "training." Does that mean he's had training or has trained others? The three words Print Production Management would have more value if total years of experience were attached. This has actually been covered in sufficient detail in the Professional Profile. There is no need to repeat that point. On a resume, you need to state things clearly once. Then go onto a new point.

The one liner, "Remote Facilities Management" would have power if David told more about the significance. Union relations are important, but those two words hardly scratch the surface. Information about what kind of union relations is valuable and needs to be stated in the work history and summed up in an overview, including information like any negotiations with unions and if he currently works as a supervisor in a union environment. Did you notice the spacing errors in the Experience section? These are common when tabs are used and show up when the resume is emailed.

Page 108 shows the resume improved.

The profile and experience were combined under one overview. This offers less for an employer to read, but what is there is more powerfully summed up and specific for the job position.

The personal pronouns were edited out. The information in the last position listed was reduced. A heading on the second page was added.

Did you notice the pattern with his training? He takes a class a year.

David Heel

788 Copper Drive
New York, NY 10023
(212)-899-5233
Heel@itis.com

PROFESSIONAL PROFILE

I'm seeking a challenging position in which I can use my management, experience, and communication skills to help an organization grow. I'm results oriented with a consistent record of exceeding standards and expectations with 20+ years of progressive print management experience. Combine strong communication and team leadership skills with exceptional motivational abilities.

EXPERIENCE

Print Production Management	Customer Service
Remote Facilities Management	Vendor Relations
Process Management & SPC	Print Estimating
Quality Control Development	Union Relations
Training	Press Checks

WORK HISTORY

TV GUIDE   1995 to Present

Operations Supervisor, New York, NY
Senior Facilities Supervisor with full responsibility of a Remote Imaging Print
Facility for TV Guide magazine. Another responsibility was for the initial build-out of this facility.

- I was Senior TV Guide Representative that managed all remote on-site Printer & Publisher issues for Quality and Manufacturing.
- I was responsible for managing a proprietary Production Control application for an Oracle database running on an Intergraph UNIX platform.
- I was responsible for all site Staffing, Network, and HR related issues.
- I managed remote site imaging of the industries first large format PostScript prepress system. Currently imaging 28 unique editions, along with 150+ 4/C files on a weekly basis.
- I handled Prepress system that images 7,500 pages of fully imposed plate ready film within a 72-hour production window. Maintain magazine integrity through internal Quality auditing system.
- I developed a Spare Parts Database for system wide use in keeping fifteen Optronics XL imagesetters running. This database can be used to locate parts nationally when an imagesetter experiences a mechanical failure.
- I developed some SOP's which were then stored on WAN Lotus Notes database that employees could use as a reference for manufacturing information.

Walker   1978-1995
<u>Prepress Supervisor</u>, Chicago, IL (1990-1995)
Walker is a 300MM printer with headquarters in Chicago, IL. This position
included scheduling, inventory, vendor contact, billing, hiring, employee
relations and general troubleshooting, etc.

- Supervised a commercial prepress department with at least 70 or more employees in a Union environment. Among the product mix was Time, People, Woman's World, and Newsweek magazine.
- Over 9,000 plates were produced per month.
- Responsible for estimating any potential new customer work.
- Developed archive system that was used for managing and the storage and the retrieval of files used in the production of Sears catalogs.

<u>Customer Service Representative</u>, (1987-1990)
Managed the accounts of ten other CSR's during the evening. Part of this job included all customer contact, and included final responsibility for all products coming off 20 web offset presses. This was the final checkpoint for millions of press impressions each day.

<u>Image Assembler/Management Trainee</u>, (1978-1987)
I was an Image Assembler before moving into a company that sponsored program in which individuals were selected for hands-on training in all areas of the corporation. These areas included all manufacturing and corporate departments.

EDUCATION

Chicago University (1978)
Major: Business Administration
Minor: Economics

Chicago Technical College (1976)
Associate Arts - Publishing

<u>Computer Skills:</u> Windows 95, 98, & NT, Word, Excel, Lotus Notes, SGI, Intergraph Workstation, and UNIX.

<u>Training:</u>
Integrated Process Management Training 2002
X-Rite Techniques of Densitometry & Quality Control 2000
Seminars International Employee Performance 2001
DuPont STOP Safety Training 1999
Facilitators Training 1998
Transformation of American Industry Training (SPC) 1997
Journal Stockholders Council Chairman - Education Committee 1996

DAVID HEEL

788 Cooper Drive
New York, New York 10023
Home: (212)-899-5233
heel@itis.com

OVERVIEW:

- Twenty plus years of progressive print management including remote facilities management.
- Results oriented with a consistent record of exceeding standards and expectations.
- Strong communication and team leadership skills with exceptional motivational abilities.
- Supervision experienced in a union work environment.

PROFESSIONAL EXPERIENCE:

TV GUIDE – Mazomanie, WI   1998–Present
One of three facilities across the country that print and bind *TV Guide* on a weekly basis.

* *Operations Supervisor*

Senior Facilities Supervisor with full responsibility of a remote imaging print facility for *TV Guide* magazine. Responsible for the initial build-out of this facility.

- *TV Guide* representative responsible for managing all remote on-site printer and publisher issues regarding quality and manufacturing.
- Responsible for managing a proprietary production control application residing on an Oracle database running on an Intergraph UNIX platform.
- Handled all site staffing, network, and HR related issues.
- Managed remote site imaging of the industries first large format PostScript prepress system. Currently imaging 28 unique editions, along with 150+ 4/C files on a weekly basis.
- Ran a prepress system that images 7,500 pages of fully imposed plate ready film within a 72-hour production window.
- Maintained magazine integrity through internal quality auditing system.
- Developed a spare parts database for system wide use in keeping fifteen Optronics XL imagesetters running. The database is used to locate parts nationally when an imagesetter experiences a mechanical failure.
- Developed SOP's which were stored on WAN Lotus Notes database that employees could reference for manufacturing information.

Chapter 5

<u>*Walker — Chicago, IL*</u>   <u>*1980–1998*</u>
A \$300M printer of periodicals and catalogs.

* *Prepress Supervisor (1990–1998)*

Supervised a commercial prepress department with 70+ employees in a union environment. Product mix included *Time, People, Woman's World,* and *Newsweek* magazine.
- Handled scheduling, inventory, vendor contact, billing, hiring, employee relations, and general troubleshooting.
- Produced over 9,000 plates per month.
- Responsible for estimating new customer work.
- Developed archive system for managing the storage and retrieval of files used in the production of Sears catalogs.

* *Customer Service Representative (1987–1990)*

- Managed the accounts of ten other CSR's, including all customer contact, and final responsibility for all products coming off of 20 web offset presses. This was the final checkpoint for millions of press impressions each day.

* *Image Assembler/Management Trainee (1980-1987)*

- Trained in all areas including manufacturing and corporate departments.

<u>*EDUCATION:*</u>

BA, Business Administration, Economics minor, Chicago University, Chicago, IL, 1978
AA, Publishing, Chicago Technical College, Chicago, IL, 1976

<u>*COMPUTER SKILLS:*</u>

Windows 95, 98, & NT; Word; Excel; Lotus Notes; SGI; Intergraph Workstation; and UNIX

<u>*TRAINING:*</u>

Integrated Process Management Training, 2002
X-Rite Techniques of Densitometry and Quality Control, 2001
Seminars International Employee Performance, 2000
Dupont STOP Safety Training, 1999
Facilitators Training, 1998
Transformation of American Industry Training (SPC), 1997
Journal Stockholders Council Chairman — Education Committee, 1996

Rule 7

Don't Mix Fonts or be Sloppy With White Space, and Make Sure Your Information Connects.

Fonts:

Look at the Paula Homes resume on page 110.

This resume is a mixture of different fonts. Some people try and do this for emphasis. Mixing fonts can be a minefield of trouble. The first problem is if you slip and are not consistent in tagging "like" material, the desired effect of the overall resume is lost. Another problem is that there is an entire science concerning the mixing of fonts on a page. Unless you've studied that science, or happen to have a unique talent for balancing text, you can create an unappealing design that actually inhibits the transfer of the information you need to easily convey.

In Paula's resume, she has most of the headings in Ariel, however, she missed using Ariel for the heading, "Special Courses." That heading is in Bookman Old Style. The job titles are in Bell MT, except she forgot to use Bell MT for her job title at Skyline Labs. That job title is also in Bookman Old Style. In general, the mixture of fonts tends to jar the eye and reduce a persons ability to quickly read the material. Select one font for the entire resume and stick with that font. You can increase size, use bold, italic, underline, or indentations for emphasis.

Don't use all capitols for emphasis of various words in a sentence. This jars the eye. Paula has done this with her words pesticide and pharmaceutical. She is better to emphasis those issues in an overview with the statement, "Over 15 years experience in pesticide analysis and over 10 years in pharmaceutical assay."

Email Address:

There are two email addresses available on this resume. Although more than one phone number is fine to leave an employer (make sure you identify them) don't put more than one email address on a resume. Unlike a phone number, the employer isn't expecting you to pick up and talk immediately. Employers don't want to guess which one you will most likely check most often. Usually it is safer to put down the home email unless a work email can be done without any employer review.

There is a bad page break between the first and the second page. Information needs to be grouped together. Never separate the company and position from the rest of the information. Insert a page break and put it all on the second page.

The personal information needs to be left off.

The lack of a different indentation for the job title and the job description/accomplishments makes the job title hard to pick out at a glance.

Paula Homes

170 Fairchild Street
Westminster, Colorado 80030
Home: (303) 488-3012
alwaysworking@aol.com
Paula@Analytical.com

OVERVIEW:

- Effective manager with strong people skills.
- Well organized, detail oriented, able to handle fast-paced projects with accuracy.
- Strong instrumentation background.
- Personal—Forty-six years old, married, two grown children.

PROFESSIONAL EXPERIENCE:

Analytical Development Corp.—Colorado Springs, CO   *1990–Present*
* *Research Scientist (1998–Present)*
- PESTICIDE AND PHARMACEUTICAL analysis, including method development, method validation and routine assay.
- Written and oral communication with clients and report writing.
- Responsible for organizing projects and meeting project deadlines.
- Supervision of technicians.

* *Research Assistant (1990–1998)*
- PESTICIDE AND PHARMACEUTICAL analysis and routine assay.
- Instrumentation expertise included high performance liquid chromatography using a UV detector, gas chromatography using electron capture and flame ionization detector/packed, Megabore, and capillary columns, gas chromatography/mass spectrometry, Harvey and Packard biological material oxidizers and the radioactive plate material oxidizers and the radioactive plate scanner.
- Techniques in 14C-radioassay and drug residue analysis of blood samples.

United States Geological Survey—Arvada, CO   *1985–1990*

* *Organic Chemist, Water Quality Laboratory*

- Preparation and analysis of priority pollutants including PESTICIDES in water and sediment samples using wet lab techniques and gas chromatography.
- Responsible for sample coordination and results reporting.

Pikes Peak Institute of Health Careers—Colorado Spring, CO   1980–1985
* *Teacher*
- Taught medical laboratory assistants basic sciences including inorganic and organic chemistry, physics, and chemical arithmetic.
- Selected new textbooks to be used for organic chemistry and chemical arithmetic.
- Wrote curriculum outlines for all courses to meet state requirements.

Skyline Labs—Wheatridge, CO   *1978–1980*
* *Chemist*
- Mineral analysis of rock and soil samples.

EDUCATION:
BS, Chemistry, Metropolitan State College, Denver, CO, 1978

SPECIAL COURSES:
Hewlett-Packard Short Course in Basic Gas Chromatography
Finnigan Interpretation of Mass Spectra
Finnigan 4000 Operator Course
Varian NMR Short Course

The Correct Use of White Space is a Science

Take a look at the Tom Allwood resume on page 114.

The spacing between Experience Record and the work history is annoyingly large and looks like the words belong more to the objective information rather than as a heading for what follows. Effective use of white space is an art and a science, and although not everyone knows how to effectively use it, most people quickly wince when white space is used poorly. Tom's resume is a good example of poor use. Scanning down the page is a jarring experience. This resume has no flow at all to lead the eye. The formatting style offered in Chapter 4 in this book will prevent you from turning out resumes that use white space poorly. The jarring effect and disconnection effect results from the poor use of white space. There is more space between his first place of employment and the others that follow, leading the eye to group information that doesn't belong together.

The resume is in Book Antiqua, which is an excellent choice; unfortunately the largest font size is 10 point, which is used for heading material, and the rest is in 9 point. The very smallest you can use with Book Antiqua is 10.5 point, and that is not recommended. The recommended minimum is 11 1/2 point. Smaller type will lose too much readability with faxing.

Tom's resume needs a date clean up by using the preferred style of year instead of month and year. The dash that is between the dates needs to be replaced with an en dash. Likewise the dash after the job title needs to be replaced with an em dash and the extra space after the dash needs to be removed.

In the heading, the phone number isn't identified as either work, home or a cell phone. A good guess is that this is a home phone; however, don't challenge an employer by making them guess about when you will most likely be available at that phone number.

The objective is a complete waste of space. We certainly hope Tom wants to pursue a graphic arts career because that is all that this resume is advertising. Objective information belongs in an interview and not on a resume.

Job Titles Need Clarification

If the Account Representative position is similar or the same as the Sales Representative position from the previous job, Tom needs to use one term consistently. When there are two job titles for the same position, you can put some additional information in to make sure that the employer knows you did the same kind of work. For instance, after the second job position of Account Representative, Tom can put the words Sales Representative in quotations. The final product would look like this:

Example

Northeast Printing Company — Albany, NY   1991–Present

* *Account Representative*

Vision Printing Company – Saratoga Springs, NY

* *Sales Representative (Account Representative)*

Another option is to re-title the Account Representative position and call both positions a Sales Representative. This is done only when the work and the similar titles are understood as equivalent throughout the industry. If in doubt, make the job titles clear.

The work history needs some rework. For instance, the sales positions would have more value with some sales figures. At American Printing, Tom needs to tell how he developed new accounts. Did he use cold calling, marketing presentations or something else? With Tom's job at Wonder Graphics, he tells us what the company does, but doesn't state any contributions he made or details about his work position.

For the most part, the information under all of the positions needs to be expanded. With a rewrite of the work history, a more active voice is needed and the personal pronouns need to be removed.

The education needs dates as to when the degrees were obtained.

The Dale Carnegie Training needs its own category. The bolding and alignment of the words Dale Carnegie Training at a glance make them appear as if they are another company he worked at.

More information that may fit with this resume is any computer experience that enhances the job position.

TOM ALLWOOD

920 Weaver Hill
Greenwich, RI 02877
(401) 899-2749

OBJECTIVE   To pursue a graphic arts career utilizing previous experience with an opportunity for professional
growth.

EXPERIENCE RECORD

10/91-Present   **American Printing Company,** Albany, NY
Account Representative – While I constantly develop new accounts, I work with management to stay in
touch with existing customer needs. This includes me marketing services so customers are knowledgeable
of how our production capabilities can be useful to them. Some of the finished items include forms, promotional
materials and stationery produced for a wide range of customers.

5/90-10/91   **Style Printing Company**, Ludlow, MA
Sales Representative – I managed existing accounts and developed new accounts from the ground up.
These included manufacturers, textbook publishing, colleges and a map maker.

7/89-5/90   **Wonder Graphics**, Portland, OR
Sales Representative – This Portland, OR based company, sold prepress services, four-color separations and
electronic systems work. It serviced accounts including ad agencies, publishers, commercial printers and packaging
printers.

5/88-7/89   **Concord Paper Company**, Albany, NY
Prepress Supervisor – I managed all prepress activities, including development of artwork and
four-color separations. I also was responsible for a three-person platemaking area where 60" lithographic
plates were exposed on a step and repeat machine. I also supervision responsibilities also included a three-
person die room where laser die-boards were fitted with scoring and cutting material so finished cartons
could be punched out of the printed sheets.

6/85-5/88   **Artmaster Press Company**, Albany, NY
Production Manager – I directed and scheduled work for four departments including prepress, press,
bindery and shipping. I worked directly with customer service and sales, purchased paper, planned and
and monitored all work until completion.

4/83-6/85   **Smith Printing Company**, East Greenville, PA
Customer Service Representative – I managed NEWSWORLD Magazine and HEALTH
accounts in all planning, production and shipping related matters and acted as primary liaison between
GARDEN WORLD, Inc. and Smith Printing Company. I serviced the publisher by resolving quality control
problems and communicating progress of each week's production.

EDUCATION   **Albany Institute of Technology**, Albany, NY
            Bachelor of Science Degree - Printing Management.

The University at Albany, Albany, NY
            Liberal Arts.

            Dale Carnegie Training, Computer Applications

Make Sure Your Information Connects

Take a look at Jack Nelson's Resume on page 116. He has created some problems with margins that are too narrow. Small margins (less than .08 inch) not only affect the transfer of faxed material, they affect emailed material. With faxed material, the sides and tops are cut off when the margins are not wide enough. With email, the information will not print on the original page. Words like Overview that were too close to the edge on Jack's resume ended up on a third page when his resume was printed from an email. On top of the second line, the word experience was lost.

Don't ask an employer to track across the page to connect company names with dates. On this resume, the combination of tabbing and narrow margins creates disjoined information. The company has become completely disconnected from the employment dates. This almost creates the need for an employer to play a different kind of match game. Putting part of the company information on the left side of the page, and the rest of the company information on the right when it is separated by a lot of white space and tiny fonts makes associating that information a challenge because the information becomes visually disconnected.

Example

If your material is spread apart like the following:

IBM — Ute, CO   **1996–Present**

Look at the product under print preview. If the information is not easily connected, change the style to the following:

IBM — Ute, CO, 1996–Present

However, once you choose a style, don't mix the styles. Don't mix the first IBM example with the second on a resume. If part of your company information is small enough to look disconnected, put all of your company information in the style shown in the second example.

Other problems include missing information. Jack failed to include his address and phone on the resume. Jack may not have initially worried about this because he was asked by a job recruiter to email his resume, however he still needs to include his address and contact phones for the recruiters to use in a database and for the resume when it is sent to the client.

Overall, too much of the work information about this individual is either missing or will take a lot of effort to connect due to lack of spacing in the work history. Jack did try to switch back and forth from Book Antiqua and Garamond to separate different areas, and used capitalization for emphasis, but without consistent spacing, the significance of the information is hard to determine. Other areas that should be separate look connected. Education looks like part of the work history instead of standing out as its own category. The use of capitalization and italics is inconsistent. In addition, his interests and objective needs to be left out.

Take a look at the final resume for Jack on page 118. The entire resume is brief and to the point. Could this final resume have been more complete with more information? If Jack were sending out the resume to many different companies he knew little or nothing about, more information may be warranted. This resume was tailored to a specific company and worked fine to land him the job.

Jack Nelson

tive
_____

to obtain a sales position with a firm that will allow me to utilize my experience and relationships in the graphics industry

to become a member of an internet firm who is involved in the printing industry

to provide security to my family

ce
_____

August 1999 – Present
Star-Webb Printing Company

Account Executive
Assigned to American Express account to sell direct mail and sheetfed
Trained on Print.com

October 1998 - April 1999
                    Top Form Graphics

Account Executive
Assigned to First Bank Account
Sold Sheet Feed, Web and Specialty Packaging

May 1998 - October 1999
                    Wilson Folder Service

Owner/Operator
Took control after my Sister's recent death
restored profitability and credibility
prepared/ positioned for future action (growth or sale)

September 1987 - April 1998
                    Vermont Graphics
started as bindery person and resigned as TOP SALES PERSON

87-89   General bindery operator (folders, cutters et.)
89-93   Bindery Manager, responsible for all bindery at Classic for this period of explosive growth, added foil stamping and diecutting
93-94   SALES TRAINING, worked on live production in striping, E-Prep, and 6 months in estimating using PSI software
95-98   ACCOUNT EXECUTIVE
95 sales of $ 890,463   No CSR, primarily Ad Agencies
96 sales of $2,064,208   1 CSR, 85%Agencys,15% Banks
97 sales of $3,019,720   1 CSR, 85% Banks, 15% others

98 sales goals 4 million a year set and sales as of April 30th were $2,019,320

consistently exceeded sales goals
increased sales by over 1 million dollars a year
150% increases in First Bank Work for two years
Coordinated a successful effort to be placed on the PREFERRED PRINT VENDOR LIST at First Bank in six months
Arranged a very successful client event at DISCOVERY PLACE for 350 First Union Print Buyers and employees
1998 sales goals were 110% higher that the next highest Sales Person

Interest	Fly Fishing, Wildlife Rehabilitation, Travel, Skiing, Printing Industry of Connecticut
Education	High School Graduate Attended Graphic Arts Program at CPCC

Mac Training in Quark, Pagemaker and Photoshop from DESKTOP TECHNOLOIGIES (TAZ TALLY)

JACK NELSON

875 Porter Road
Greenwich, Connecticut 06831
Home: (203) 622-1842

OVERVIEW:

- Up to speed with newest on-line printing technologies.
- Strong affiliations with commercial printing for the banking industries.
- Consistently exceeds sales goal.
- Over ten years experience in printing industry.
- Strong experience in direct mail and sheet fed sales.

PROFESSIONAL EXPERIENCE:

Star Printing Company — West Port, CT   *1999–Present*
Commercial printer based in New York. Office in West Port specifically dedicated to serving the banking industry.

* *Account Executive*

- Sells direct mail and sheet fed printing to American Express.
- Built account from 1M gross per year to 5M.
- Uses on-line printing technologies including Print.com and NOOSH.

Top Form Graphics — New York, NY   *1998–1999*
High-quality Commercial Sheet fed printer.

* *Account Executive*

- Assigned to Prospect the First Union Account
- Sold Sheet Feed, Web and Specialty Packaging
- Resigned when PBM failed to achieve "Preferred Vendor" Status with First Union.

Wilson Folder Service — Westport, CT   *1998–1999*
Charlotte-based trade shop, owned by relative.

* *Owner/Operator*

- Assumed control following sister's death. Restored profitability.
- Positioned company for sale.

<u>*Vermont Graphics — Burlington, VT*</u>   <u>*1987–1998*</u>
$15M, Commercial Sheetfed printer.

In the last full year with Classic Graphics, sales were in excess of $3M. The vast majority of the business was direct sales to the banking industry. Resigned as #1 Salesperson, tracking to exceed $4M.

* *Account Executive (1995–1998)*

  - Consistently exceeded sales goals; consistently increased sales by $1M per annum.
  - 150% increase in sales from First Bank account.
  - Coordinated a successful effort to be placed on the Preferred Print Vendor List at First Bank in six months.

* *Sales Trainee (1993–1994)*

* *Bindery Manager (1989–1993)*

* *General Bindery Operator (1987–1989)*

EDUCATION:

AA, Graphic Arts, West Port Community College, West Port, CT, 1986.

OTHER COURSES:

Quark 1998
PageMaker 1998
PhotoShop 1998

INDUSTRY AFFILIATION:

Printing Industry of Connecticut

Chapter 6

Dealing With Too Much or Too Little on a Resume

Some candidates have a lot of very impressive information on their resumes. Editing down the volume into two pages is challenging. Even a neat, well-organized resume that at first glance appears professional and appealing can lose out to the competition when too much information taxes the reader. Information overload causes a complete failure in communicating the best skills of the candidate. This chapter deals with reducing work descriptions down to the most powerful and pertinent information. Also addressed in this chapter are job histories that can give the wrong impression if not handled correctly. For candidates who are dealing with too sparse of information on a resume, examples are given to help to learn how to fill in the missing information.

Guidelines for Reducing Information on a Resume

- Rearrange the resume correctly and format the resume using the final font and style to better gage the total amount of information.
- Analyze the work history to determine what is the most valuable to an employer.
- Revise the most important work history first.
- Reduce the least important work history. Typically the least important is not relevant to the current position, was worked at only a short period of time, or was worked a very long time ago and more current work history is more relevant.

Jeff Hansen Resume Analysis

The Jeff Hansen resume is on page 121. At first glance, this resume looks professional and well-organized, but it has some problems that will turn away employers. Three and a half pages is a fairly long resume and this resume is deceptively longer. When the 9 and 10 point, Times New Roman font is changed to a better size of 12 point Book Antiqua, the resume spans five pages. Part of the excess length is because the work history needs to be directed to better show his strengths. Instead of doing this job in his work history, Hansen chose to do it in a summary he titled Business Competencies. This is the wrong approach. For most employers, work history is where employees show their real value. An overview or summary should never be used to substitute for showing accomplishments that belong in the work history itself. Since this resume is loaded down with job information that merely documents what Hansen did at his various jobs, it is hard to quickly determine Hansen's true value as an employee. The sheer density of the material works against Hansen by burying his strongest qualities in unnecessary repetition found throughout the work history. This means an employer will need to take a lot of time to access Hansen's strong points and true value as a candidate. These days few employer have that kind of time.

ORIGINAL RESUME

Jeffery R. Hansen
Jeff@hotmail.com

924 Sparrow Drive
Chicago, Illinois 60516

Home: (815) 620-9241
Office: (815) 620-7914

Profile

Over twenty years of experience in international and US marketing and sales for document printing and business communications. A proven track record of developing innovative and successful business strategies. Extensive experience in product management, research and development, direct and distributor channel marketing, strategic and tactical business planning, customer relationship management, customer communications and training. A successful, customer-focused leader who actively coaches others for service and optimum results.

Business Competencies

Management
- Assemble and manage effective cross-functional teams for product, for services and for systems development.
- Motivate and challenge others to succeed.
- Develops and effectively manages large budgets
- Develops and executes winning business plans.
- Establishes metrics and performance benchmarks to manage individuals, projects and business results.
- A creative and practical problem solver.
- Interact very comfortably and effectively with all managerial and functional areas.
- Improves business processes. Optimum organizer.

Marketing
- Develops strategic marketing programs and systems that drive and support customer relationship management products and services.
- Develops and implements strategic marketing plans and tactical elements that deliver successful business results.
- Develops and manages winning training and communication. Drive sales growth while reinforcing brand recognition.
- Extensive experience in product & services development, planning, and marketing.
- Obtains winning results.
- Establishes strong competitive market positioning.
- Establishes business alliances and marketing programs that enhance product, service and support offerings.
- Establishes concepts and ideas that lead to innovation / improvement of competitive products, services and systems.
- Creatively integrates multiple technologies and services.
- Develops new revenue streams and deliver sound customer solutions.
- Delivers tangible sales results through effective sales & marketing campaigns.

Professional Experience

2002 - Present Westside Print.com, Chicago, IL.

Channel Marketing
Responsible for developing all marketing programs specifically geared to attract, recruit and manage reseller channels for selling an internet based ASP print management and e-procurement application targeted at fortune 500 companies.
- Develop, negotiate and manage reseller contracts.
- Developed the joint business planning process.
- Led the joint business planning process to establish financial goals, strategic and tactical sales & marketing activities geared to drive growth.
- Led development of self-directed training program geared to drive product & service awareness among reseller organizations.
- Developed all partner recruiting collateral material.
- Develop customized collateral and direct mail marketing programs geared to drive sales among reseller client base.
- Successfully negotiated reseller agreements with major North American digital print company, procurement consortium, print and workflow consulting firm, and asset management software firm.

1999 to 2002 Horizon *(Formerly Jasper Business Systems Div.)* **Chicago, Illinois**

Director, Services Marketing (US Operations)
Responsible for driving development of technology solutions to support the company's document management, direct marketing and response management initiatives.

♦ Directed the development and management of new Internet enabled systems for print management. These services enabled customers to directly transact business with the company. New Internet solutions also supported the companies sales associates by enabling access to internal systems for submission of orders remotely. Internet systems are key to supporting Horizon cost reduction initiatives, driving account penetration and new account acquisition.

♦ Led new business venture in response management services to support the company's direct marketing and customer relationship management initiatives. Oversaw professional cross-functional team for development of web-enabled response management services, budgeting, business planning, system architecture, technology and services development, service center set-up, market positioning, market rollout, sales compensation and training.

♦ Collaborated with industry leading customer relationship management consulting firm to develop and introduce company's response management business.

1998 - 1999 Dun-Moore, Inc., Eastern Ontario *(Canadian operations of Horizon)*

Vice President, Marketing (1.6 yr. Assignment)
Appointed to this position on an interim basis. Responsible for all aspects of Canadian marketing operations including business planning, product management for a $150 million line of products & services. Handled R&D, corporate communications and direct marketing. Was offered the position full time but declined due to regional location.

♦ Appointed to this position following Jasper acquisition of Dun-Moore.

♦ Restructured business development department and created a professional marketing organization. Managed a product management team, corporate communications, R&D team, and a direct marketing sales development team.

♦ Generated over $2 million in new sales in ten months and reduced non-recoverable R&D costs by 80% through the implementation of a new customer directed R&D process.

♦ Delivered a 50% increase in sales and an 10% margin improvement in directs fiscal sales.

♦ Hired a business unit general manager and developing a marketing strategy to improve flat sales.

♦ Delivered an 20% physical increase in outsourced product sales and a 4% margin improvement through initiation of a trade relations program with internal capabilities.

♦ Positioned the company as a single source supplier of print and related products and services.

♦ Slowed sales erosion of a major $20 million stock product line by 50% over prior year and increased margins by 4% through implementation of an aggressive sales and marketing program.

♦ Developed and implemented a demand print marketing and technical training program. This contributed to a 50% year over year sales increase and a 4% margin improvement.

1995 – 1998 Horizon *(formerly Jasper Business Systems Div.),* **Chicago, Illinois**

Director of Product Marketing & Advanced Document Systems (US Operations)
Built and managed a professional product management team. Responsible for integrating product and services acquired through acquisition and expanding a $500 million product line. Responsibilities included product/services planning & development, collateral and campaign development, marketing rollouts, sales training and technical support.

♦ Promoted to this position after building the core marketing processes in the prior year.

♦ Actively engaged in five division acquisitions. Directed all product marketing related integration activities (Jordan Graphics, Duplex Products, Vanier Graphics, Dun-Moore).

♦ Directed the development and rollout of several key product lines including a commercial printing which resulted in sales increased 70% over two years. Document security products including check writing software solution which resulted in a sales increased of 90% over 2 years. Handled Mailer Products which increased sales 90% in the first year and improved margins 10%.

♦ Conceived of and initiated traveling sales symposiums that include product/service training seminars and vendor trade shows. Symposiums are fully supported by the company's trade relations and marketing teams and is a key vehicle used for product and services education.

1992 –1995 Horizon *(formerly Jasper Business Systems Div.)*, **Chicago, Illinois**

Manager, Product Marketing

Responsible for a $150 million product line. Drove all product marketing activities including product planning, development, product performance and reporting and marketing rollouts.

♦ Developed business processes for planning and development, collateral development and training and market rollouts.

♦ Developed a new product/service coding system to enable tracking and measurement of product sales

♦ Developed new sales and promotional tools where few previously existed. Strategically positioned and supported product & service sales while establishing a corporate brand identity.

♦ Provided technical service, support and sales training to the sales organization on key products and services.

♦ Worked with operations, engineering, finance, legal, and pricing to drive key product initiatives through the development cycle

♦ Created competitive price levels.

1991 – 1992 Spartan Business Communications, Inc. Dayton, Ohio

Executive Director, Sales and Marketing

(Parent company Paragon sold company to Hunter Company in 1992 and closed operations)

Recruited to the company as part of a business turnaround initiative. Led the company's sales, marketing and customer service initiatives including sales management, product management, customer service and order entry.

♦ P&L responsibility for $10 million product line.

♦ Developed and conducted a market research study to determine customer perceptions of Spartan products, quality, services and value. Implemented new customer service and order entry processes geared to enhance quality, service and delivery.

♦ Initiated new order management processes and refocused the sales force on selling *solutions and services* rather than product as a means of driving product sales.

♦ Delivered a 20% physical increase in sales and an 12% increase in margins through establishment of performance objectives and benchmarks.

♦ Increased customer service productivity 25% and reduced order entry staffing 15% through implementation of an order entry system.

♦ Introduced variable printing technology to the company and acquired ink-jet imaging capabilities to broaden the product and service. Reached break-even point in four months and went onto ramp-up digital printing business to a $1 million run rate in the first eight months.

1986 – 1991 Bedford Corporation, New York, New York

Marketing Manager

♦ Responsible for management of self-mailer systems and integrated specialty products. Handled R&D, product rollouts and training.

♦ Developed the business plan and spearheaded development and introduction of the *QuickSeal* laser compatible self-mailer system. This was the first fully laser compatible mailer system introduced to the US market. First year sales exceeded $1.5 million.

♦ Negotiated a third party equipment partnerships with Pitney Bowes for the development of processing equipment required for the QuickSeal system.

♦ Established strategic business and marketing partnership programs with major technology firms. Tested products with digital printing technologies and created resale agreements for system distribution.

♦ Developed and introduced 12 new stock mailer and label products contributing to 25% physical growth in stock sales over 2yrs.

♦ Developed sales and marketing collaterals and promotional campaigns to drive independent distributor sales of company products and services.

1984 – 1986 Topco & Company, New York, New York

Product Marketing Manager, New Products & Research, DocuSystems Group.

♦ Responsible for market research, development and product & services for transportation and financial markets.

1978 – 1984 Fountain Business Forms, Inc., Willow Springs, Illinois
♦ Progressed through the ranks starting as a Product Specialist. Worked up to Product Marketing Manager for several product lines which included a $35 million mailing system and a $20 million line of selected in-house manufactured and subcontracted products.

Computer/Software Skills
MS Word, Windows 2000, WordPerfect, Lotus Ami Pro, Freelance, PowerPoint, Excel, WebEx Internet presentation tools, Power Internet User

Education
Undergraduate School: Concordia University of Wisconsin, Madison, Wisconsin, - Bachelors Degree in 1978 in Marketing / Psychology

Continuing Education Courses:
Negotiating Skills – Olson Training Institute
Power Based Selling – Olson Training Institute
Counselor Sales Person Training, Phoenix University
Diversity Management, Phoenix University
Strategic Planning - Phoenix University
Dale Carnegie Public Speaking & Human Relations

STEP 1: Reformat the Resume

The first step in revising Jeff's resume was to put it into a larger font so that the actual length of the information could be gauged. The Profile and Business Competencies sections were then removed because they will be summarized after the work history is redone. To get a better perspective on the work history, the company name and employment dates were made more clear. Look at the reformatted version below. The font is now Book Antiqua, 12 point, and the information has been rearranged to more accurately show the work history.

> When revising a resume, don't worry about creating bad page breaks. You will address those problems when you create the final version.

JEFFERY R. HANSEN

924 Sparrow Drive
Chicago, Illinois 60516
Home: (815) 620-9241
Office: (815) 620-7914
Jeff@hotmail.com

PROFESSIONAL EXPERIENCE:

Westside Print.com—Chicago, IL   *2002–Present*

* *Channel Marketing*

Responsible for developing all marketing programs specifically geared to attract, recruit and manage reseller channels for selling an internet based ASP print management and e-procurement application targeted at fortune 500 companies.

- Developed, negotiated and managed reseller contracts.
- Developed the joint business planning process.
- Led the joint business planning process to establish financial goals, strategic and tactical sales & marketing activities geared to drive growth.
- Led development of self-directed training program geared to drive product & service awareness among reseller organizations.
- Developed all partner recruiting collateral material.
- Developed customized collateral and direct mail marketing programs geared to drive sales among reseller client base.
- Successfully negotiated reseller agreements with major North American digital print company, procurement consortium, print and workflow consulting firm, and asset management software firm.

Horizon (Formerly Jasper Business Systems Div.) – Chicago, IL   **1992–2002**

* *Director of Marketing Services (1999–2002)*

Responsible for driving development of technology solutions to support the company's document management, direct marketing and response management initiatives.

- Directed the development and management of new Internet enabled systems for print management. These services enabled customers to directly transact business with the company. New Internet solutions also supported the company's sales associates by enabling access to internal systems for submission of orders remotely. Internet systems are key to supporting Horizon cost reduction initiatives, driving account penetration and new account acquisition.
- Led new business venture in response management services to support the company's direct marketing and customer relationship management initiatives. Oversaw professional cross-functional team for development of web-enabled response management services, budgeting, business planning, system architecture, technology and services development, service center set-up, market positioning, market rollout, sales compensation and training.
- Collaborated with industry leading customer relationship management consulting firm to develop and introduce company's response management business.

* *Vice President of Marketing – Canadian Operations/Dun-Moore Div. (1998–1999))*

- Appointed to this position on an interim basis. Responsible for all aspects of Canadian marketing operations including business planning, product management for a $150 million line of products & services. Handled R&D, corporate communications and direct marketing. Was offered the position full time but declined due to regional location.
- Appointed to this position following Jasper acquisition of Dun-Moore.
- Restructured business development department and created a professional marketing organization. Managed a product management team, corporate communications, R&D team, and a direct marketing sales development team.
- Generated over $2 million in new sales in ten months and reduced non-recoverable R&D costs by 80% through the implementation of a new customer directed R&D process.
- Delivered a 50% increase in sales and a 10% margin improvement in direct fiscal sales.
- Hired a business unit general manager and developed a marketing strategy to improve flat sales.
- Delivered a 20% physical increase in outsourced product sales and a 4% margin improvement through initiation of a trade relations program with internal capabilities.

- Positioned the company as a single source supplier of print and related products and services.
- Slowed sales erosion of a major $20 million stock product line by 50% over prior year and increased margins by 4% through implementation of an aggressive sales and marketing program.
- Developed and implemented a demand print marketing and technical training program. This contributed to a 50% year-over-year sales increase and a 4% margin improvement.

* *Director of Product Marketing and Advanced Document Systems (1995–1998)*

Built and managed a professional product management team. Responsible for integrating product and services acquired through acquisition and expanding a $500 million product line. Responsibilities included product/services planning & development, collateral and campaign development, marketing rollouts, sales training and technical support.

- Promoted to this position after building the core marketing processes in the prior year.
- Actively engaged in five division acquisitions. Directed all product marketing related integration activities (Jordan Graphics, Duplex Products, Vanier Graphics, Dun-Moore).
- Directed the development and rollout of several key product lines including a commercial printing which resulted in a 70% sales increase over two years, and document security products including check writing software solution which resulted in a sales increased of 90% over 2 years. Handled Mailer Products, which increase sales 90% in the first year and improved margins 10%.
- Conceived of and initiated traveling sales symposiums that include product/service training seminars and vendor trade shows. Symposiums are fully supported by the company's trade relations and marketing teams and are a key vehicle used for product and services education.

* *Product Marketing Manager (1992–1995)*

Responsible for a $150 million product line. Drove all product marketing activities including product planning, development, product performance and reporting, and marketing rollouts.

- Developed business processes for planning and development, collateral development and training, and market rollouts.
- Developed a new product/service coding system to enable tracking and measurement of product sales
- Developed new sales and promotional tools where few previously existed. Strategically positioned and supported product & service sales while establishing a corporate brand identity.

- Provided technical service, support and sales training to the sales organization on key products and services.
- Worked with operations, engineering, finance, legal, and pricing to drive key product initiatives through the development cycle.
- Created competitive price levels.

Spartan Business Communications, Inc. — Dayton, OH   *1991–1992*

Parent company Paragon sold company to Hunter Company in 1992 and closed operations.

* *Executive Director of Sales and Marketing*

Recruited to the company as part of a business turnaround initiative. Led the company's sales, marketing and customer service initiatives including sales management, product management, and customer service and order entry.

- P&L responsibility for $10 million product line.
- Developed and conducted a market research study to determine customer perceptions of Spartan products, quality, services and value. Implemented new customer service and order entry processes geared to enhance quality, service and delivery.
- Initiated new order management processes and refocused the sales force on selling *solutions and services* rather than product as a means of driving product sales.
- Delivered a 20% physical increase in sales and a 12% increase in margins through establishment of performance objectives and benchmarks.
- Increased customer service productivity 25% and reduced order entry staffing 15% through implementation of an order entry system.
- Introduced variable printing technology to the company and acquired ink-jet imaging capabilities to broaden the product and service. Reached break-even point in four months and went on to ramp-up digital printing business to a $1 million run rate in the first eight months.

Bedford Corporation — New York, NY   *1986–1991*

* *Marketing Manager*

Responsible for management of self-mailer systems and integrated specialty products. Handled R&D, product rollouts and training.

- Developed the business plan and spearheaded development and introduction of the *QuickSeal* laser compatible self-mailer system. This was the first fully laser compatible mailer system introduced to the US market. First year sales exceeded $1.5 million.
- Negotiated a third party equipment partnership with Pitney Bowes for the development of processing equipment required for the QuickSeal system.

- Established strategic business and marketing partnership programs with major technology firms. Tested products with digital printing technologies and created resale agreements for system distribution.
- Developed and introduced 12 new stock mailer and label products contributing to 25% physical growth in stock sales over 2 years.
- Developed sales and marketing collaterals and promotional campaigns to drive independent distributor sales of company products and services.

Topco & Company, New York, NY   *1984–1986*

*   Product Marketing Manager—New Products and Research*

Responsible for market research, development and product and services for transportation and financial markets.

Fountain Business Forms, Inc.—Willow Springs, IL   *1978–1984*

Progressed through the ranks starting as a Product Specialist. Worked up to Product Marketing Manager for several product lines, which included a $35 million mailing system and a $20 million line of selected in-house manufactured and subcontracted products.

COMPUTER/SOFTWARE SKILLS:

MS Word, Windows 2000, WordPerfect, Lotus Ami Pro, Freelance, PowerPoint, Excel, WebEx Internet presentation tools, Power Internet User

EDUCATION:

BS, Marketing, minor in Psychology, Concordia University of Wisconsin, Madison, WI, 1978

CONTINUING EDUCATION COURSES:

Negotiating Skills—Olson Training Institute, 1997
Power Based Selling—Olson Training Institute, 1994
Strategic Planning—Olson Training Institute, 1993
Counselor Sales Person Training—University of Phoenix, 1987
Diversity Management—University of Phoenix, 1986
Dale Carnegie Public Speaking & Human Relations, 1983

* _ * _ * _ * _ * _ *

STEP 2: Analyze the Work History

Jeff has a lot of information in his work history, which spans four pages. Jeff needs to communicate himself in just two pages, part of which will have to include his name, address and other contact information, and his education. Jeff basically needs to tell his work history in about a page and a half. This means he needs to make choices about what best sells him to an employer.

Jeff's Resume Goal

To know what to include in a resume, the raw material (presented by Jeff as his original resume) needs to be scrutinized. Each achievement and accomplishment needs to be looked at with respect to its relevance to portraying him as a candidate for the position he now seeks. Each part of his work history must contribute to building him as a viable candidate, and what is left after editing must not exceed two pages.

A Synopsis of Jeff's Resume

One way to get a feel for what is important about Jeff's work history is to sum it up as if you were in charge of briefly telling a hiring manager all about Jeff. The following is a synopsis of Jeff's resume:

- Starting at the end of the resume, one can see that Jeff graduated in 1978 with a bachelor of science degree in marketing.
- He went to work the same year at Fountain Business Forms where he worked his way from Product Specialist to Marketing Manager in six years.
- Next, he worked at Topco for two years as a Product Marketing Manager.
- He worked at Bedford for five years as a Marketing Manager. While there, his first year's sales exceeded $1.5M. He did sales and marketing, R&D, product rollouts, and training. He developed and introduced 12 new stock mailer and label products, contributing to a 25% increase in stock sales over two years.
- He had a job at Spartan for about a year.
- His work at Horizon was his strongest work history. He started as a Product Marketing Manager, did that for three years, and then was a Director of Product Marketing and Advanced Products for three years.
- Jeff's history reveals that he excelled at Horizon when he was appointed Vice President of Marketing. The company had a division in Canada that they had recently acquired. Jeff transferred there and turned around a company with eroding sales by generating $2M in sales in only ten months. He reduced non-recoverable R&D costs by 80% and delivered a 50% increase in sales and a 10% margin improvement in direct fiscal sales. Then he delivered a 20% physical increase in outsourced product sales and a 4% margin improvement with a trade relations program. Jeff positioned the company as a single-source supplier of print and related products. This part of his work history demonstrates his abilities when he is in charge. He states that this was an interim position, and that he turned down a full-time appointment due to location.
- Jeff went back to being Director of Marketing Services at Horizon, and stayed at the company for about two years. He then took his current job at Westside Print.com as a Channel Marketing Manager, but he shows no sales figures for this job.

Jeff's resume gives equal space to most of his positions. His most important position as VP of Marketing at Horizon gets only a few more lines than the others. If space and employer reading time were not issues with which the resume-writer must be concerned, this fact wouldn't matter very much. But space and employer reading time *are* major issues. Jeff needs to give the most space to his most important job positions. Doing so will help an employer with limited time to focus in on Jeff's best qualities. Also, the reworked resume needs to make his greatest accomplishments far more prominent than they were in the original resume. The final resume must accent those accomplishments by giving them the most space.

Step 3: Revise the Work History

Start With The Most Important Work History First

The most important position is revised first because after it is finished, it will show you exactly how much space remains. The rest of the history will be contained in the available space. Due to space limitations, some of the work history will be reduced to no more than a company and job title. As with any part of the work history, the most important job history needs to be tightened up and reworked until all the words have strong impact, each point is clearly made, and points are expressed only once.

To begin the rewrite of Jeff's work history, start with the position in which he had the greatest accomplishments. Typically the most recently held position is the most important. Exceptions to this general rule can include when the most recent position wasn't held long enough for the candidate to have made significant contributions. Another exception is when the most recent job is in a field other than the field in which the candidate is seeking a job. Jeff's current position is one that he wants to leave. He's been there a relatively short time, and he has no sales figures or other major accomplishments. For Jeff, as we saw in the previous section, his most significant position is not his most recent position. Instead, his most significant position was as Vice President of Marketing at the Canadian office of Horizon. Here is the way Jeff originally stated that position in his resume.

Vice President of Marketing—Canadian Operations/Dun-Moore Div. (1998–1999)

- Appointed to this position on an interim basis. Responsible for all aspects of Canadian marketing operations including business planning, product management for a $150 million line of products & services. Handled R&D, corporate communications and direct marketing. Was offered the position full time but declined due to regional location.
- Appointed to this position following Jasper acquisition of Dun-Moore.
- Restructured business development department and created a professional marketing organization. Managed a product management team, corporate communications, R&D team, and a direct marketing sales development team.
- Generated over $2 million in new sales in ten months and reduced non-recoverable R&D costs by 80% through the implementation of a new customer directed R&D process.

- Delivered a 50% increase in sales and a 10% margin improvement in direct fiscal sales.
- Hired a business unit general manager and developed a marketing strategy to improve flat sales.
- Delivered a 20% physical increase in outsourced product sales and a 4% margin improvement through initiation of a trade relations program with internal capabilities.
- Positioned the company as a single source supplier of print and related products and services.
- Slowed sales erosion of a major $20 million stock product line by 50% over prior year and increased margins by 4% through implementation of an aggressive sales and marketing program.
- Developed and implemented a demand print marketing and technical training program. This contributed to a 50% year-over-year sales increase and a 4% margin improvement.

Make a Point Only Once

Repetition in a resume needs to serve a purpose. That purpose is to show consistency in work history. Repetition that says the same thing in a slightly different way loads down the employer with reading without the benefit of new or unique information. A common mistake seen on some resumes is to take the same point and restate it a slightly different way. Jeff does this in his first two lines. His first bulleted position states he was appointed to this position on an interim basis. In the very next bullet, he again states he was appointed to this position, but adds that the appointment came after the Jasper acquisition of Dun-Moore. This restatement has an added disadvantage in that another company name needs to be deciphered with regard to where it is significant in connection with his accomplishments. An employer has to stop and figure out who and what role Jasper plays in this whole event. Jasper's role does nothing to communicate Jeff as a viable candidate and needs to be eliminated.

The rewritten work history is shown below. Grammatical edits have also been made.

* **Vice President of Marketing — Canadian Operations/Dun-Moore Div. (1998–1999)**

Responsible for all aspects of this newly acquired division, including business planning, R&D, corporate communications, direct marketing, and product management for a $150 million line of products and services. Appointed on an interim basis and was offered the position full-time. Declined due to regional location.

- Generated over $2M in new sales in ten months and reduced non-recoverable R&D costs by 80%.
- Delivered a 50% increase in sales and a 10% margin improvement in direct fiscal sales.

- Delivered a 20% physical increase in outsourced product sales and a 4% margin improvement through initiation of a trade relations program with internal capabilities.
- Positioned the company as a single-source supplier of print and related products and services.
- Slowed sales erosion of a major $20M stock product line by 50% over prior year and increased margins by 4% through an aggressive sales and marketing program.
- Developed a demand-print marketing and technical training program that contributed a 50% year-over-year sales increase and a 4% margin increase.

A well-written work history makes the candidate's duties stand out as important or critical to the company where the candidate worked.

This part of the resume now shows how Jeff took over a newly acquired division and did well. The fact that Horizon offered him a permanent position demonstrates his employer's approval of his accomplishments.

Work to Reduce the Least Important Work History

Only Include What is Most Important About the Job

The rest of Jeff's job history needs to be refined to fit on the resume. What needs to be included is the information that quickly illustrates and supports Jeff's progress as a worker. The strongest points in his job history include his career as a Product Specialist and his position as Vice President of Marketing. Those areas need to be well-represented when the resume is redone.

Reducing Information From the Least Important Jobs

When tackling job information reductions, start at the least important position first. That is usually the last position listed in the job history. Jeff shows his career starting at Fountain Business. At that company, he went from Product Specialist to Product Marketing Manager. More recent jobs on the resume can show his abilities and accomplishments as a Product Marketing Manager so it is sufficient just to show the job titles at Fountain Business Forms because the work was done almost twenty years ago.

The next job, at Topco & Company, was also as a Product Marketing Manager. Jeff only worked there two years, and this job was held close to 20 years ago. Therefore for this job, all that is shown is the company name and the job title. Room is thus preserved for accomplishments at more recent positions.

Jeff's next position at Bedford Corporation as Marketing Manager spanned five years. A few highlights are mentioned.

Although he only worked at Spartan Business Communications for a few years, Jeff felt it was important and significant to note his achievements as an Executive Director of Sales and Marketing.

Returning to the Most Important Company's Work History

After Spartan, Jeff went to work at Horizon. At the time, the business had a different name, and that is noted on the company line on the resume. At Horizon, Jeff started as a Product Marketing Manager, became Director of Product Marketing and Advanced Document Systems, was appointed Vice President of Marketing, and then returned for a brief time to work as Director of Marketing Services.

Because the Product Marketing Manager position was the least important of the four positions, and because space didn't permit elaboration, only the title is listed. A few accomplishments are shown for the Director of Product Marketing and Advanced Document Systems, and for the Director of Marketing Services. Cuts were painfully made. Only the most significant items were retained.

Also removed from the resume were the continuing education courses and Jeff's computer skills. For a Vice President of Manufacturing, this information is not as important as what is preserved in the limited space in his work history.

The Final Resume

In the final resume on page 135, grammatical errors were corrected and an Overview added. Note that in the final resume, Jeff's ten-year work history at Horizon appears on the first page. The first page of any resume has the most impact. Having this information here gives Jeff a strategic advantage. At a glance, Jeff's positions as Vice President of Marketing stands out. Although the demands of a two-page resume mean the work history must be brief, Jeff's strongest points still come through. To fit in the Overview, additional space reduction techniques were used. Those techniques are covered in Chapter 8.

FINAL RESUME **JEFFERY R. HANSEN**

924 Sparrow Drive
Chicago, Illinois 60516
Home: (815) 620-9241
Office: (815) 620-7914
Jeff@hotmail.com

OVERVIEW:

- Over twenty years of experience in international and US marketing and sales for document printing and business communications.
- A proven track record of developing innovative and successful business strategies that deliver profitable sales growth.
- Extensive experience in product management, research and development, direct and distributor channel marketing, strategic and tactical business planning, customer relationship management, and customer communications and training.

PROFESSIONAL EXPERIENCE:

Westside Print.com — Chicago, IL   *2002–Present*

* *Channel Marketing Manager*

Develop marketing programs for reseller channels to sell Internet-based ASP print management and e-procurement applications targeted at Fortune 500 companies.

Horizon (Formerly Jasper Business Systems Div.) — Chicago, IL   *1992–2002*

* *Director of Marketing Services (1999–2002)*

Drove marketing programs for new Internet-enabled systems for print management. Managed cost reduction initiatives, account penetration, and new account acquisition.

* **Vice President of Marketing — Canadian Operations/Dun-Moore Div. (1998–1999)**

Responsible for all aspects of this newly acquired division, including business planning, R&D, corporate communications, direct marketing, and product management for a $150 million line of products and services. Appointed on an interim basis and was offered the position full time. Declined due to regional location.

- Generated over $2M in new sales in ten months and reduced non-recoverable R&D costs by 80%.
- Delivered a 50% increase in sales and a 10% margin improvement in direct fiscal sales.
- Delivered a 20% physical increase in outsourced product sales and a 4% margin improvement through initiation of a trade relations program with internal capabilities.
- Positioned the company as a single-source supplier of print and related products and services.

- Slowed sales erosion of a major $20M stock product line by 50% over prior year and increased margins by 4% through an aggressive sales and marketing program.
- Developed a demand-print marketing and technical training program that contributed a 50% year-over-year sales increase and a 4% margin improvement.

* *Director of Product Marketing and Advanced Document Systems (1995–1998)*

Expanded a $500M product line after acquisition of five divisions.

- Increased sales 70% over two years through development and rollout of several key product lines, including commercial printing. Increased sales 90% with check writing security products and mailer products.
- Initiated traveling sales symposiums including product/service training seminars and vendor trade shows.

* *Product Marketing Manager (1992–1995)*

<u>*Spartan Business Communications, Inc.—Dayton, OH*</u>   <u>*1991–1992*</u>

* *Executive Director of Sales and Marketing*

Led the company's sales, marketing, and customer service initiatives for a $10 million product line focusing on solutions and services rather than product to drive the sales.

- Delivered a 20% physical increase in sales and a 12% increase in margins through establishment of performance objectives and benchmarks.
- Increased customer service productivity 25% and reduced order entry staffing 15% with new order entry system.
- Introduced variable printing technology to the company and acquired inkjet imaging capabilities. Reached a $1M run rate in the first eight months.

<u>*Bedford Corporation—New York, NY*</u>   <u>*1986–1991*</u>

* *Marketing Manager*

Handled self-mailer systems and integrated specialty products.

- Introduced the *QuickSeal* system. The first-year sales exceeded $1.5 million.
- Contributed to 25% growth over two years with introduction of stock mailers.

<u>*Topco & Company, New York, NY*</u>   <u>*1984–1986*</u>

* *Product Marketing Manager—New Products and Research*

<u>*Fountain Business Forms, Inc.—Willow Springs, IL*</u>   <u>*1978–1984*</u>

Started as a *Product Specialist* and worked up to *Product Marketing Manager*.

EDUCATION:

BS, Marketing, minor in Psychology, Concordia Univ. of Wisconsin, Madison, WI, 1978

Arthur Monroe Resume Analysis

Look over Arthur's original resume on page 138. He is a talented and bright individual, but was getting poor responses from his resume. His resume needs to be redone to eliminate some problems. What appears to be a three-page resume is actually four solid pages when the font is changed to a more readable and faxable size. The Objective section wastes space and the Education section belongs on the last page, not the first, as does the rest of the current first-page information.

At first glance, Arthur's work history indicates he has had problems keeping a job. The beginning of his resume shows that the most recent job lasted only about a year and a half, the next job lasted about a year, and the third job lasted less than a year. Employers who glance at the work history will most likely write Arthur off as a job-hopper or a problematic employee. If the job dates don't discourage a potential employer, the tiny, 10-point font that describes his work experience and accomplishments probably will. In actuality, Arthur is not a job-hopper or a problematic employee. While his cover letter addresses his circumstances, often resumes and cover letters become separated when the resume is analyzed. It is imperative that Arthur's resume present his work experience in such a way that he does not appear to be a job-hopper.

The Goals for Arthur Monroe's New Resume

- His current resume presents his information in a non-conventional way by putting his educations and technical skills first. This needs to be corrected.
- His consulting information needs to be correctly presented. It currently appears as if he held several unrelated jobs. Consulting can be considered as one job and the various locations can be presented as if they were job titles.
- Arthur needs to reduce the overall size of his total content and bring out his most valuable assets.
- The job-hopping appearance needs to be eliminated.

ORIGINAL RESUME

Arthur D. Monroe

150 W. Sombrero Dr.	Santa Fe, NM 80234	505-871-9189

Email: Arthur@hotmail.com

Objective:
To obtain a position that is challenging and utilizes my broad knowledge base and experience.

Education:
UNIVERSITY OF COLORADO AT DENVER
B.S. in Electrical Engineering, GPA 3.5, May 1997

Certifications:
Cisco Certified Network Associate (CCNA)

Technical Skills:

Operating Systems: UNIX (Solaris 2.x), LINUX, Windows 95/98/00, Windows NT Server/Workstation

Languages: ANSI C, C++, HTML, UNIX Shell, Perl & Expect Scripts w/vi editor, Procomm/ASPECT Scripts

Applications: HP Openview NNM, SunNet Manager, MS Office, Visio, and Procomm Plus

Networking Protocols: TCP/IP, ATM, SNMP, Ethernet, Bridging, Switching, Routing (OSPF, RIP, IGRP)

Networking Equipment: Cisco Routers – 1600, 2500, 4000, 4500, 3600, & 7000 series.
Cisco ATM Switches – BPX
Cisco Ethernet Switches – Catalyst 2900 & 5000 series.
Cisco DSLAM– 6100 & 6130
Copper Mountain DSLAM– CE200
N-Base (formerly Xyplex) – 1620 & 1640 Terminal Servers & 9000 Chassis.
Applied Innovations – AI180, AI130, AIScout & AIM Chassis.
Alcatel (former Xylan equipment) – Omni 3, 5 & 9 Chassis.

Training:

Solaris 2.X System Administration
Advanced UNIX
Advanced Cisco Router Configuration
Cisco BPX Switch and Services Configuration
ATM Internetworking
Xylan Switch Expert
Applied Innovation (180NAII-4IF)
SunNet Manager
HPOV NNM for Windows NT
Introduction to DSL

PROFESSIONAL EXPERIENCE

Baker Netconnections Inc.   Santa Fe, NM

•Senior Network Engineer   December 2002 – August 2003

Worked as a member of the Engineering Support Group to assist Operations Teams in resolving network issues by looking at root causes that may be technology related and providing tier 4 support. Facilitated additional engineering knowledge transfer by recognizing areas where additional training or technical procedures from the Engineering Team would be beneficial. Functioned as the Development Engineering Team's point of contact for the Operations Team's escalations, allowing for quicker resolution of network issues that arose.

Accomplishments:

- Worked as a member of the Fault Reduction Team to analyze recurring problems, determine the root cause of those problems and provide input to vendors on the solutions to those problems. This resulted in cost savings for the company, more satisfied customers and more efficient day-to-day operation within the Rhythms NOC.

- Built Procomm/Aspect and UNIX scripts to assist in analyzing trend analysis and to automate equipment upgrades using SNMP.

Simple Products Inc.   Raleigh, NC & Denver, CO

•Senior Engineering Consultant   September 2001 – October 2002

Provided customers with network engineering, architecture and implementation services and support. Worked with customers to evaluate, design and/or upgrade their network infrastructure. Provided project management of the network installation. Documented troubleshooting procedures as well as the engineering specifications of their network infrastructure. Provided training on a variety of network technologies and equipment to include Cisco routers and Xyplex terminal servers. Provided clients with custom software packages.

Accomplishments:

- Provided turnkey engineering and implementation services to Time Warner Telecom's OSS group enabling their NOC to do remote surveillance and provisioning. Assisted in Cisco router upgrades to improve network performance and security. Provided training on a variety of OSS related technologies and equipment. Built UNIX scripts to assist engineers in automating some of their day-to-day activities.

Netion Systems (formerly Enterprise Engineering Inc.)   Denver, CO

•Consultant   March 2001– September 2001

Provided customers with network engineering, architecture and implementation services and support. Worked with customers to engineer, install and test upgrades and additions to their network infrastructure. Built UNIX scripts to assist in network installations and upgrades. Documented troubleshooting procedures as well as the engineering specifications of their network infrastructure.

Accomplishments:

- Inventoried and documented Qwest Communications' entire OSS network infrastructure. Provided recommendations on necessary changes that needed to be made to improve network efficiency. Worked with Qwest personnel on the implementation of these changes. Upgraded network equipment for Y2K compliance. Built Unix scripts to automate day-to-day activities and to query network equipment for statistics and configurations.

Time Warner Telecom   Greenwood Village, CO

•OSS Network Engineer   January 1997 – February 1999

Engineered and managed the installation of a nationwide OSS/IT network infrastructure. Configured and maintained OSS and IT networking equipment including high-end Cisco routers, Cisco FDDI/CDDI concentrators, Cisco Ethernet repeaters and switches, Xyplex terminal servers and AI Switches. Maintained configuration documentation. Provided high level troubleshooting on router, frame relay, X.25 and TCP/IP problems. Implemented network security with router access lists and firewalls. Evaluated and optimized local and wide area networks for capacity and speed. Coordinated with Network Applications Group for alarm visibility in the National Operations Center. Evaluated new vendor products such as ATM switches, Ethernet hubs and switches, routers, and modems.

•Sr. Data Network Engineer   February 1999 – January 2001

Engineered, configured and managed installation of metropolitan area ATM networks using Xylan OmniSwitches and PizzaSwitches used to provide transparent LAN services to Time Warner Telecom customers. Designed and implemented a management platform using HP Openview Network Node Manager and Xylan XVision to provide alarm and remote provisioning capabilities into the NOC. Developed testing and troubleshooting procedures for this network.

Accomplishments:

- Engineered and managed the transition of Time Warner's entire core network infrastructure to a new location with no down time while simultaneously improving network efficiency.

- Designed and constructed an Intranet Web server to store and update all OSS engineering documentation by the use of forms and C programs. Also created Unix/Expect scripts used to automate recurring tasks such as equipment password changing and network discovery.

- Designed and implemented network security policies and procedures using router access lists and firewalls.

University of Colorado at Denver   Denver, CO

•Network Technician   May 1996 - December 1996

Installed and maintained network hubs and wiring including fiber-optic and twisted-pair for 10-baseT connections. Installed and maintained interface cards and needed software for PCs and Macintosh personal computers.

Headquarters Air Force Satellite Control Facility   Sunnyvale, CA

•Satellite Systems Operator   June 1995 - January 1996

Maintained and operated ten Varian 75 mainframe computers used for transmitting and receiving data for more than fifty defense satellites and for NASA's space shuttle program. Trained, supervised and evaluated new personnel. Scheduled equipment and maintained pertinent records.

•Network Interface Data Systems Operator   May 1994 - January 1995

Configured and operated four Varian 77 mainframe computers and associated patch panels. Established data line contact for the transmission and reception of data between remote locations. Operated Codex 6030 and 6040 Intelligence Network Processors. Responsible for running line check diagnostic procedures to isolate failing equipment.

References available upon request.

Step 1: Reformat the Resume

A good way to approach rewriting is to remove unnecessary information, rearrange the information, and then reformat the resume to better view the important information. For Arthur's resume, the Objective section and the statement about references being available are removed. Those items don't belong on a resume. The work history is then moved to the beginning, and other sections are moved to the end. For the job at Time Warner, the chronological order is incorrect. The most recent position always appears first. Finally, the font is changed to Book Antiqua 12-point, and the formatting is changed to correspond to the formatting described in Chapter 4. Now we have a better idea of what Arthur's work history actually contains.

ARTHUR D. MONROE

150 W. Sombrero Dr.
Santa Fe, New Mexico 80234
Home: 505-871-9189
Arthur@hotmail.com

PROFESSIONAL EXPERIENCE:

Baker Netconnections Inc. — Santa Fe, NM   *2002–2003*

* *Senior Network Engineer*

Worked as a member of the Engineering Support Group to assist Operations Teams in resolving network issues by looking at root causes that may be technology related and providing tier 4 support. Facilitated additional engineering knowledge transfer by recognizing areas where additional training or technical procedures from the Engineering Team would be beneficial. Functioned as the Development Engineering Team's point of contact for the Operations Team's escalations, allowing for quicker resolution of network issues that arose.

- Worked as a member of the Fault Reduction Team to analyze recurring problems, determine the root cause of those problems and provide input to vendors on the solutions to those problems. This resulted in cost savings for the company, more satisfied customers and more efficient day-to-day operation within the Rhythms NOC.
- Built Procomm/Aspect and UNIX scripts to assist in analyzing trend analysis and to automate equipment upgrades using SNMP.

Tangible Products Inc. — Raleigh, NC and Denver, CO   *2001–2002*

* *Senior Engineering Consultant*

Provided customers with network engineering, architecture and implementation services and support. Worked with customers to evaluate, design and/or upgrade their network infrastructure. Provided project management of the network installation. Documented troubleshooting procedures as well as the engineering specifications of their network infrastructure. Provided training on a variety of network technologies and equipment to include Cisco routers and Xyplex terminal servers. Provided clients with custom software packages.

- Provided turnkey engineering and implementation services to Time Warner Telecom's OSS group, enabling their NOC to do remote surveillance and provisioning. Assisted in Cisco router upgrades to improve network performance and security. Provided training on a variety of OSS related technologies and equipment. Built UNIX scripts to assist engineers in automating some of their day-to-day activities.

Netion Systems (formerly Enterprise Engineering Inc.) — Denver, CO   _2001_

* _Consultant_

Provided customers with network engineering, architecture and implementation services and support. Worked with customers to engineer, install and test upgrades and additions to their network infrastructure. Built UNIX scripts to assist in network installations and upgrades. Documented troubleshooting procedures as well as the engineering specifications of their network infrastructure.

- Inventoried and documented Qwest Communications' entire OSS network infrastructure. Provided recommendations on necessary changes that needed to be made to improve network efficiency. Worked with Qwest personnel on the implementation of these changes. Upgraded network equipment for Y2K compliance. Built UNIX scripts to automate day-to-day activities and to query network equipment for statistics and configurations.

Time Warner Telecom — Greenwood Village, CO   _1997–2001_

* _Sr. Data Network Engineer (1999–2001)_

Engineered, configured and managed installation of metropolitan area ATM networks using Xylan OmniSwitches and PizzaSwitches used to provide transparent LAN services to Time Warner Telecom customers. Designed and implemented a management platform using HP Openview Network Node Manager and Xylan XVision to provide alarm and remote provisioning capabilities into the NOC. Developed testing and troubleshooting procedures for this network.

- Engineered and managed the transition of Time Warner's entire core network infrastructure to a new location with no down time while simultaneously improving network efficiency.

- Designed and constructed an Intranet Web server to store and update all OSS engineering documentation by the use of forms and C programs. Also created UNIX/Expect scripts used to automate recurring tasks such as equipment password changing and network discovery.
- Designed and implemented network security policies and procedures using router access lists and firewalls.

OSS Network Engineer (1997-1999)

Engineered and managed the installation of a nationwide OSS/IT network infrastructure. Configured and maintained OSS and IT networking equipment including high-end Cisco routers, Cisco FDDI/CDDI concentrators, Cisco Ethernet repeaters and switches, Xyplex terminal servers and AI Switches. Maintained configuration documentation. Provided high level troubleshooting on router, frame relay, X.25 and TCP/IP problems. Implemented network security with router access lists and firewalls. Evaluated and optimized local and wide area networks for capacity and speed. Coordinated with Network Applications Group for alarm visibility in the National Operations Center. Evaluated new vendor products such as ATM switches, Ethernet hubs and switches, routers, and modems.

University of Colorado at Denver — Denver, CO   *1996*

Network Technician

Installed and maintained network hubs and wiring including fiber-optic and twisted-pair for 10-baseT connections. Installed and maintained interface cards and necessary software for PCs and Macintosh personal computers.

Headquarters Air Force Satellite Control Facility Sunnyvale, CA   *1994-1996*

Network Interface Data Systems Operator (1995-1996)

Configured and operated four Varian 77 mainframe computers and associated patch panels. Established data line contact for the transmission and reception of data between remote locations. Operated Codex 6030 and 6040 Intelligence Network Processors. Responsible for running line check diagnostic procedures to isolate failing equipment.

Satellite Systems Operator (1994-1995)

Maintained and operated ten Varian 75 mainframe computers used for transmitting and receiving data for more than fifty defense satellites and for NASA's space shuttle program. Trained, supervised and evaluated new personnel. Scheduled equipment and maintained pertinent records.

Education:
BS, Electrical Engineering, GPA 3.5, University of Colorado at Denver, 1997

Certifications:
Cisco Certified Network Associate (CCNA)

Technical Skills:
Operating Systems: UNIX (Solaris 2.x), LINUX, Windows 95/98/00, Windows NT Server/Workstation

Languages: ANSI C, C++, HTML, UNIX Shell, Perl & Expect Scripts w/vi editor, Procomm/ASPECT Scripts

Applications: HP Openview NNM, SunNet Manager, MS Office, Visio, and Procomm Plus

Networking Protocols: TCP/IP, ATM, SNMP, Ethernet, Bridging, Switching, Routing (OSPF, RIP, IGRP)

Networking Equipment: Cisco Routers – 1600, 2500, 4000, 4500, 3600, & 7000 series.
Cisco ATM Switches – BPX
Cisco Ethernet Switches – Catalyst 2900 & 5000 series.
Cisco DSLAM– 6100 & 6130
Copper Mountain DSLAM– CE200
N-Base (formerly Xyplex) – 1620 & 1640 Terminal Servers & 9000 Chassis.
Applied Innovations – AI180, AI130, AIScout & AIM Chassis.
Alcatel (former Xylan equipment) – Omni 3, 5 & 9 Chassis.

Training:
Solaris 2.X System Administration
Advanced UNIX
Advanced Cisco Router Configuration
Cisco BPX Switch and Services Configuration
ATM Internetworking
Xylan Switch Expert
Applied Innovation (180NAII-4IF)
SunNet Manager
HPOV NNM for Windows NT
Introduction to DSL

Step 2: Analyze the Work History

Now that the work history is reorganized, we can more easily see the details of Arthur's work experience as follows:

- Arthur worked at Baker for about a year.
- He worked at Simple Products about a year as a consultant.
- He worked at Netion less than a year as a consultant.
- He worked at Time Warner for four years. This is his most notable job. He started as an OSS Network Engineer and worked up to Senior Data Network Engineer.
- The last part of the work history details jobs that were done while Arthur was in school. Although these were regular jobs and not internships, they are not as important as jobs he held after graduation.

Deciding What to Emphasize

Arthur accumulated good work experience while he was in school, and then put his talents to work at Telecom. He was downsized after Telecom merged with Time Warner. This started him on a rough employment path. He did consulting work until he found permanent work at Rhythms, but unfortunately Rhythms went bankrupt, leaving him to look for a new job again. His current resume doesn't communicate that he is a strong employee chiefly because of his frequent job changes. Also, his current resume gives equal emphasis to each position at which he worked. That creates two problems. First, it makes his resume far to long. Second, it doesn't readily communicate his real strengths. Work history needs to feed an employer information about what your strong points are without asking the employer to digest densely-packed information. Because Arthur's strongest job position is his work experience at Time Warner/Telecom, he needs to make that experience stand out more than his other positions.

Step 3: Revise the Work History

Rework the Most Important Job First

The first step in revising Arthur's job history is reworking his most important position. That is the Time Warner/Telecom position. The information needs tightening by removal of redundant information. The rule of thumb is to say it once, say it well, and only say it if the information is specifically what the employer needs to know to determine if you are a viable candidate.

Reduce Job History Information

Reduce the less important information to give the most emphasis on his strongest job positions. For the first job at Rhythms, since he was there only a short period of time, information can be trimmed. He needs to tighten what he states to show only what is significant. Other areas that can be reduced are the jobs he held while earning his degree. When no other work experience is available, this information is preserved, however Jeff has some solid work that he accumulated after he graduated. The work he did after graduation better represents his abilities.

Handling Consulting Job Information

Consulting is an honorable profession. Some people take on a consulting position for a number of years, while others use consulting work as a way to remain employed until they get a more viable job. Arthur's original resume shows that he had two consulting positions. The way he presents the information on his original resume, however, makes it appear as if he had two permanent jobs that only lasted a short period of time. A better way of presenting the information is listing Consulting as if it were a company name, and then listing the separate jobs with the job titles as if they were a different division of the same company. Make sure the consulting work dates are synchronous when they are grouped together.

Resolving the "Job Hopping" Appearance

Handling the consulting information correctly did a lot to help resolve the appearance that Arthur was a job-hopper. He still had the misfortune, however, of having two important jobs end due to either bankruptcy or merger. Although it is not recommended to state in the job history why you left a particular job, it is sometimes advantageous to elaborate about the company history in a way that allows an employer to realize why you may no longer be working at that company. If you use this technique, use it sparingly and with great discretion. For Arthur's resume, a short explanation now appears under his most recent job that explains why he no longer works there. The reason is implied, rather than directly stated.

Bending the Rules

We have seen that Arthur's resume has a few examples of stretching and bending the rules. The final rule that he will bend is the one about keeping his resume to two pages in length. For some people, technical skills, certifications, training and other special categories alone can take up an entire page. When this information is critical to your presentation of yourself as a viable employee, you can include a third page in your resume. Be sure that your work history and other information is edited to fit in the first two pages though, and that only special categories appear on the third page.

The Final Resume

Look at Arthur's final resume on page 147, and see how he now comes across as a more appealing candidate. One unfortunate disadvantage of his final resume presentation was that his work at Time Warner Telecom appeared on the second page instead of the first. Because his work at Time Warner Telecom was the strongest part of his work history, there would have been an advantage to having it on the first page. The alternative is to have it at the very top of the second page. The statement "Telecom Merged with Time Warner in 2001" doesn't say why Arthur left the company, but an employer may well guess that he lost his job due to the merger or a downsizing. The reason Arthur no longer works at WorldCom is alluded to by the statement: "WorldCom acquired company's assets after Rhythm's bankruptcy in 2003."

FINAL RESUME   **ARTHUR D. MONROE**

150 W. Sombrero Dr.
Santa Fe, New Mexico 80234
Home: 505-871-9189
Arthur@hotmail.com

OVERVIEW:

- Over six years of experience as a Network Engineer doing design, project lead and management, documentation, installation, and cabling services.
- Expertise in high-level engineering, design, testing, and troubleshooting of both LAN and WAN network infrastructures, including Cisco routers and switches.
- Strong UNIX skills, including scripting and system administration.
- Excellent communications skills at all levels of management and customers.
- Accustomed to large-scale projects that involve managing employees and vendors, project management, budget management, and large-scale network engineering and configuration.

PROFESSIONAL EXPERIENCE:

Rhythms Netconnections Inc. — Englewood, CO   2002–2003
WorldCom acquired company's assets after Rhythms' bankruptcy in 2003.

* *Senior Network Engineer*

- Provided tier-4 support as a member of the Engineering Team, which provided faster resolution of technology-related issues.
- Analyzed recurring problems and provided input to vendors on the solutions, which resulted in cost savings, greater customer satisfaction, and more efficient day-to-day operation.
- Built ProComm/Aspect and UNIX scripts to assist in problem trend analysis and automation of equipment upgrades using SNMP.

Senior Engineering Consultant   2001–2002

* *Tangible Products Inc. — Raleigh, NC and Denver, CO (2001–2002)*

- Provided turnkey engineering, implementation, and consulting services to Time Warner Telecom's OSS group. Provided formal training on a variety of network technologies and equipment. Provided clients with custom software packages.

* *Netion Systems — Denver, CO (2001)*

- Inventoried and documented Qwest Communications' entire OSS network infrastructure. Developed troubleshooting procedures. Recommended upgrades and changes.
- Built UNIX scripts to automate day-to-day activities and to query network equipment for statistics and configurations.

Arthur D. Monroe   *Page 2*

<u>*Time Warner Telecom — Greenwood Village, CO*</u>   <u>*1997–2001*</u>
(Telecom Merged with Time Warner in 2001)

* *Sr. Data Network Engineer (1999–2001)*

- Engineered and managed the transition of Time Warner's entire core network infrastructure to a new location with no downtime while simultaneously improving network efficiency.
- Engineered, configured, and managed installation of metropolitan area ATM networks using Xylan switches that provided transparent LAN services to Time Warner Telecom customers.
- Designed and implemented a management platform using HP Openview NNM and Xylan XVision to provide alarm and remote provisioning capabilities into the NOC. Also developed testing and troubleshooting procedures for the network.
- Evaluated new vendor products such as ATM switches, Ethernet hubs and switches, routers, and modems.

* *OSS Network Engineer (1997–1999)*

- Engineered and managed the installation of a nationwide OSS/IT network infrastructure, including configuration and maintenance of Cisco routers and switches. Maintained configuration documentation.
- Provided high-level troubleshooting on router, frame relay, X.25, and TCP/IP problems.
- Designed and implemented network security policies and procedures using router access lists and firewalls.
- Evaluated and optimized local and wide area networks for capacity and speed.
- Coordinated with Network Applications Group for alarm visibility in the National Operations Center.
- Designed and constructed an intranet Web server to store and update all OSS engineering documentation.
- Developed UNIX and Expect scripts used to automate recurring tasks such as equipment password changing and network discovery.

<u>*University of Colorado at Denver — Denver, CO*</u>   <u>*1996*</u>

* *Network Technician*

<u>*Headquarters Air Force Satellite Control Facility — Sunnyvale, CA*</u>   <u>*1994–1996*</u>

* *Network Interface Data Systems Operator (1995–1996)*

* *Satellite Systems Operator (1994–1995)*

Arthur D. Monroe   *Page 3*

EDUCATION:

BS, Electrical Engineering, GPA 3.5, University of Colorado at Denver, 1995.

CERTIFICATION:

Cisco Certified Network Associate (CCNA)

TECHNICAL SKILLS:

Operating Systems: UNIX (Solaris 2.x), LINUX, Windows 95/98/2000, Windows NT Server/Workstation

Languages: ANSI C, C++, HTML, ProComm/ASPECT Scripts, UNIX Shell, Perl and Expect Scripts w/vi editor,

Applications: HP Openview NNM, SunNet Manager, MS Office, Visio, ProComm Plus

Network Protocols: TCP/IP, ATM, SNMP, Ethernet, Bridging, Switching, Routing (OSPF, RIP, IGRP)

Network Equipment: Cisco Routers — 1600, 2500, 4000, 4500, 3600, and 7000 series
Cisco ATM Switches — BPX
Cisco Ethernet Switches — Catalyst 2900 and 5000 series
Cisco DSLAM – 6100 and 6130
Copper Mountain DSLAM — CE200
N-Base/Xyplex/iTouch — 1620, 1640 and 9000 Chassis
Applied Innovations — AI180, AI130, AIScout and AIM Chassis
Alcatel (former Xylan equipment) — Omni 3, 5 and 9 Chassis.

TRAINING:

Cisco BPX Switch and Services Configuration — Ascolta Training Co., 2001
Introduction to DSL — Rhythms Netconnections, 2001
HPOV NNM for Windows NT — HP Educational Services, 1998
Xylan Switch Expert — Xylan Corporation, 1997
Interpersonal Managing Skills — Time Warner Telecom, 1997
ATM Internetworking — American Research Group, 1997
Solaris 2.X System Administration — Sun Microsystems, 1997
Advanced UNIX — American Research Group, 1996
SunNet Manager — The Root Group, 1995
Applied Innovation (180NAII-4IF) — Applied Innovation, 1995
Advanced Cisco Router Configuration — Cisco Systems, 1995

Dealing With Too Little on a Resume

Guidelines for Filling Out the Resume

- Check into the qualifications the employer is looking for and make sure they are included on your resume.
- Be sure to thoroughly describe the important parts of the job where you worked. Check help wanted ads to see what skills are typically listed for that or similar positions.
- Include skills and talents that help present you as a well rounded employee. Those skills and talents might include awards that are relevant to your job, or special training such as first-aid training.
- Don't forget to include a summary of your job history in the form of an Overview.

Worley Analysis

The Alden Worley resume on page 151 needs to be fleshed out. The qualifications need to be assigned to the work history, and the computer skills and other training needs to be placed in their own sections. Also, the work history must have dates for each position.

Techniques to Help In Filling Out the Work History

- Sit down and list what you do on a daily basis, or a weekly basis, or a monthly basis. Not all this information will not be included, but writing all of it down can help you shape the emphasis of the description of your job.
- Write a job description as if you were writing the job requirements for your replacement.
- Sometimes you can get ideas by doing a web search for similar positions to see what qualities are emphasized in the job descriptions.
- Some people find it easier to talk when they are not writing. If that is true for you, try using a tape recorder to voice your ideas. Then you can type them out from your recording.
- Look up an ad for a similar job, or find the job description the company has for your position. Also check out the job requirements for a similar job you are hoping to fill.
- Go to a web page for the company and read about the company you hope to send the resume to.

The Final Resume

Although the revised resume shows information about his work as a Lettershop Manager in two jobs, something this book has said to avoid, in this case showing the information is acceptable. A resume that doesn't have a lot of work description or a lot of accomplishments can repeat information about very similar jobs in order to show consistencies and length of experience. In a resume with many accomplishments, those accomplishments are dependent upon certain work skills, and therefore those work skills aren't always mentioned because of space limitations. But in smaller, simpler resumes, the repetition is fine. The revised resume is shown on page 152.

ORIGINAL RESUME
Alden Worley

420 Thatch Street
Cleveland, Ohio 44111
Home: (216) 452-6847
Al@Hotmail.com

Objective

Provide a company with my expertise of more than ten years experience in direct mailing, with a proven track record of supporting all corporate activities.
Utilize administrative skills. Offer consistent, organized, highly motivated effort along with the dedication necessary to build a career.

Qualifications

Management of people
Hiring and firing of people
Keeping accurate records
Payroll
Balancing postal permit accounts
Maintaining a relationship with the post office
Know how to operate a gavern, meter machines, a folder, an inkjet, and an inserter.

Work History

Ohio Direct Mailing, Cleveland, OH - Lettershop Manager

Responsible for 35 people and running the lettershop.
Use computer programs like Microsoft Office, Lotus 1-2-3 and Word Perfect.

Mailing Services Inc., Pittsburgh, PA -Lettershop Manager and Operator

Responsible for 80 employees and 46 inserting machines.

Schooling in lettershop management at Midwest College. Went between 1987 and 1989 and graduated.

Also trained in CPR and advanced first-aid.

Final Resume   **Alden Worley**

420 Thatch Street
Cleveland, Ohio 44111
Home: (216) 452-6847
Al@Hotmail.com

OVERVIEW:

- Over ten years of experience in direct mailing, with a proven track record of supporting all corporate activities.
- Utilize administrative skills that involve creative and supportive techniques with a common denominator of commitment to perform quality.
- Strong knowledge of gravure, meter machines, folder, inkjet, and inserter operations and training.

PROFESSIONAL EXPERIENCE:

Ohio Direct Mailing—Cleveland, OH   *1998–Present*

* *Lettershop Manager*

Production coordinator for lettershop and laser room department supervising 35 people.
- Hire and terminate employees.
- Schedule all training.
- Keep accurate records of production.
- Review time cards for payroll.
- Maintain a relationship with the post office including balancing postal permit accounts.
- Operator of gravure, meter machines, folder, inkjet, and inserter.

Mailing Services Inc.—Pittsburgh, PA   *1990–1998*

* *Lettershop Manager and Operator*

- Managed 80 employees and 46 inserting machines.
- Hire and terminated employees.
- Reviewed time cards for payroll.
- Kept accurate records of production.
- Handled customer service, job quotations, and production scheduling.
- Balanced postal permit accounts.

Alden Worley   *Page 2*

EDUCATION:

AA, Lettershop Management, Midwest College, Cleveland, OH, 1989

COMPUTER SKILLS:

Microsoft Office
Lotus 1-2-3
Word Perfect

OTHER TRAINING:

CPR and Advanced First-Aid

Patty Hatch's Resume—The Analysis of an Office Resume.

Look at Patty Hatch's original resume on page 155. The work history is too sparse. She needs to give more detail about her responsibilities at each position.

The reworked resume shows a better presentation of her skills. The final resume was formatted so that it presents only her first two jobs on the first page. The first two jobs make a better impression than the first three would because her third job was through a temporary employment agency and of short duration.

Employers doing a quick read through a non-executive resume will often review a first page, and if they see the basics are there, flip to the second page for skills. They may only glance out of curiosity at the rest of the work history. If Patty had put her temporary employment job on the first page, it might have left the employer with a less favorable opinion then when that job was less visible on the second page.

Notice on the final resume on page 157 that the date of birth was removed. Don't put this kind of personal information on a resume.

ORIGINAL RESUME

Patty Hatch
25 Willamette
Colorado Springs, CO 90907
Home: (719) 592-6134
September 10, 1953

Education
Institution: Metropolitan State College
Degree: None
Major: General Studies

APPLICABLE EXPERIENCE

Feb. 1998 to May 2003
Privett Container

Worked as Shipping Clerk. Also helped with other office duties.

Nov. 1994 to Dec. 1997
Trimble Navigation

Worked as Administrative Assistant.
Customer calls
Messages
Shipped equipment.
Inventory
Miscellaneous office duties.

Jan. 1993 to June 1994
City of Colorado Springs

Worked as a Secretary
Phone calls
Some billing

Feb. 1990 to Jan. 1993
POSKO Custom Homes

Bookkeeping
Scheduling
Phone calls.

<u>Computer Programs Familiar With</u>

DOS, Windows 95, 98, 2000, MS Word 4.0 and 5.0, WordPerfect
MS Word for Windows, Quicken, Excel, ACT,
Word Star, Peachtree.

Final Resume

PATTY R. HATCH

25 Willamette
Colorado Springs, CO 90907
Home: (719) 592-6134
Patty@hotmail.com

OVERVIEW:

- Self-starter capable of working without direct supervision.
- Strong office experience.
- Excellent organizational skills.
- Experienced at scheduling and shipping.
- Bookkeeping experience includes accounts payable, accounts receivable, payroll, and general ledger using Peachtree and Quicken programs.

PROFESSIONAL EXPERIENCE:

Privett Container—Monument CO   *1998 to 2003*

* *Shipping Clerk*

- Responsible for shipments of corrugated boxes by truck or UPS according to schedules.
- Assisted other office personnel with billing using Peachtree.
- Assisted with other accounting tasks as time allowed.

Trimble Navigation—Castle Rock, CO   *1994 to 1997*

* *Administrative Assistant*

- Fielded customer calls and prioritized messages for sales representatives.
- Selected and shipped out equipment by Federal Express to supply needs of salespeople in the field.
- Managed the inventory of equipment using Microsoft Excel.
- Worked without direct supervision.
- Responsible for monthly sales report.

City of Colorado Springs/Accounting Dept. — Colorado Springs, CO   *1993 to 1994*
Worked through Dupont Temporary Services

* *Secretary*

  - Handled five phone lines.
  - Assisted with monthly billings.

POSKO Custom Homes — Monument Colorado, CO   *1990 to 1993*

* *Office Manager*

  - Responsible for all office tasks.
  - Scheduled subcontractors.
  - Handled phone calls.
  - Used Quicken to do bookkeeping including accounts receivable, accounts payable, post to the general ledger, and generate payroll.

COMPUTER PROGRAMS:

Microsoft Windows systems including 2000
Microsoft Word
WordPerfect
Word Star
Excel
ACT Database
Quicken
Peachtree

EDUCATION:

General Studies, Metropolitan State College, Denver, CO, 1985–1988.

Chapter 7

Specialized Resumes

Federal Resumes

Federal resumes have unique requirements. Among the items needed on a federal resume are an account number, title and grade of job applying for, Social Security number, country of citizenship, veterans preference, Federal civilian preference, high school degrees and any higher degrees with the ZIP code of the institution if known. Also usually required are the supervisor's name, telephone number and address, and whether the supervisor can or cannot be contacted. In addition, these resumes must show salaries and number of hours worked in each position, and employment history including all jobs held during the last ten years. If you plan to create a Federal resume, you need to consult a book that specializes in that format.

Functional Resumes

The functional resume presents skills, abilities, and experience without the benefit of work history. The correct use for this type of resume is when someone does freelance work for several employers and a dated work history isn't applicable. Artists, photographers, and writers often use these types of resumes. Example 7I on page 176 shows a functional resume.

This style of resume has also been used for people who had work histories that didn't readily support the job they were seeking. This kind of a resume quickly became popular with people who had something to hide in their work history. Most employers are wary when they receive a functional resume, and some will immediately dismiss the candidate presenting one.

Although a legitimate use of a functional resume is for someone who wants to change job careers, anyone with a solid work history needs to present that information. Most employers rate work history very highly when deciding to interview a candidate.

If you need a resume for a career change, the advantages of a functional resume can be obtained without omitting job history. To do this, use a large section on the first page to state applicable skills, and reduce the work history to little more than dates and company names and a few accomplishments that round you out as an employee or that can be related to the skills needed in the new profession you are seeking.

Sales Resumes

Although the basic format used in this book works well for sales resumes, sales resumes often have an advantage over other resumes. When well presented, some employers are more willing to read a paragraph containing information for sales personnel. Examples are given of what I call the "Jim" style of sales resume because Jim used this style to place a lot of sales people. If this style fits your personality, you can use it.

Examples 7A (page 161) and 7B (page 163) show some of the "Jim" style sales resumes.

College Graduates and Soon to Graduate

The best time to send out a resume for your profession is prior to graduation. The type of resume used has a specific style due to the content. Two sets of addresses and phone numbers are presented for resumes sent out prior to graduation. This is necessary because some employers will make contact prior to graduation while others will file a resume and then later call after the candidate has graduated.

Basic Format

School resumes are usually one page.

- List both your school address (if not yet graduated) and permanent address. If possible, give an email address, but be sure it is valid past your graduation date.
- State education before any work experience because the education has more value than internships done while in college. State your anticipated graduation date.
- If you took difficult coursework towards your degree, state that in a separate category, but don't bog down the resume with every little course you took.
- Mention exceptional grades.
- Be sure to list any internships you had. Give important detail without wasting space or reading time.
- If you don't have any work experience in your field of study, list regular job experience. Give a brief explanation of what you did, emphasizing anything that will help round you out as a potential employee.
- List activities and achievements that show character and that support the potential for achievement as an employee. Team sports may be included because that kind of participation shows abilities that are transferable to the workplace.

A lot of the errors in college graduation resumes include typos, spacing errors and inconsistencies in information grouping, a font size that is too small, sentences that are jarring and don't flow smoothly, and poor visual presentation of the material on the page. These problems give the resume an immature look and convey a negative image to employers, even before a single word is read.

Samples 7C (page 165) and 7D (page 166) give some examples of the appearance of pre-graduation resumes.

Example 7A

CLIFFORD R. BARTON

292 Spring Street
Naperville, IL 60565
Home: (847) 452–4802
Mobile: (847) 210–3692
Bart@Hotmail.com

EXPERIENCE:

RR Donnelley & Sons — Chicago, IL   **(1997–Present)**

RR Donnelley & Sons is a Fortune 500 corporation and the nation's premier printer of magazines, catalogs, and books.

Senior Sales Representative, Magazine Group responsible for generating new sales activities while managing existing customer base in assigned territories. Territories include Los Angeles, San Diego, and Arizona. Contributed 83% of current sales portfolio. Average 32% growth in sales last two years. Located in satellite sales office with minimal supervision. Currently manage in excess of $6M in sales, comprised of 19 customers and 60 current prospects.

Quebecor Printing — New York, NY   **(1994–1997)**

Sales Representative who was responsible for selling new accounts into regional printing plant located in Merced, CA. Led new sales two of three years. Exceeded sales budget all three years. Managed Southern California, Arizona, and Nevada territories for Merced sales. Sold $3.8M in new sales. Managed $5M in sales.

Penwell Printing — Los Angeles, CA   **(1993–1994)**

Sales Representative who called on publishers and catalogers throughout Southern California.

American Signature — Provo, UT   **(1988–1993)**

West Coast Sales Representative who covered the entire 11-state western region for this short/medium-run $20M publication printer. Worked from home for four of eight years, and then managed regional office. Grew territory from $100,000 in sales to over $5.5M. Finished in excess of 100% of assigned goals each year. Led company in new sales six of eight years. Managed 23% of all company sales.

American Signature—Costa Mesa, CA (1986-1988)

West Coast Sales Representative who called on publishers in Southern California for this short-run printer. Led the company with new sales into Dallas for 1985. Worked out of Orange County manufacturing plant and sold over $500,000 in sheetfed business.

Times Mirror Press—Los Angeles, CA (1985-1986)

Sales Representative who was hired to maintain the Donnelley directories, a $25M account. Sold $200K before the acquisition by GTE and subsequent job elimination.

EDUCATION:

AA, Business, Metro Community College, Los Angeles, CA, 1984

Example 7B

HOWARD L. CONNELL

4210 Elderwood Lane
San Juan, California 42675
Home: 949–576–2147
Howard@aol.com

PROFESSIONAL EXPERIENCE:

American Web Printing, Miami Valley Plants—San Juan, CA   **(1996–Present)**

Vice President of Sales and Marketing responsible for evaluating, reorganizing, and motivating nine people selling the print production of free-standing inserts and commercial pieces. Conceived and implemented strategies and disciplines that significantly impacted opportunities for volume and profit. Increased sales volume from $20M to a forecasted $39M in the past two years.

The Danner Press—Canton, OH   **(1990–1996)**

Vice President of Sales and Marketing who directed all phases of sales operations involving a national sales force of 14 persons. Conceived and implemented marketing plans that broadened distribution, increased sales, and achieved company turn-around that lead to six-figure profits in one year. Established major accounts; prepared and implemented long-term growth strategies, emphasizing relationship-building in the publishing and other market segments resulting in increased sales from $35M to $52M.

Northwood Inc.—Chicago, IL   **1989–1990**

Executive Vice President of Sales and Marketing for this $30M company. Provided prepress and creative graphic arts services from concept through print management. Responsibilities included marketing direction and sales-team development and management. The company changed management in 1990.

Arcata Graphics, Book Group—Arlington Heights, IL   **1985–1989**

Vice President and Regional Sales Manager—Midwest who managed major accounts and a sales force of 12 in four locations. Developed non-traditional market segments and staff-building program. Sales achievements resulted in growth from $37M in 1988 to $48M in 1990. Designed and implemented partnership with General Motors Photographic (Detroit) as major subcontractor for catalog production. Opened new Detroit-area sales/support office. Increased catalog business by adding three major accounts in the chemical industry totaling $3M+ in annual sales. Developed and initiated Elementary/High School marketing strategy that was implemented company-wide and resulted in significant sales increases. Developed Canadian publishing market, aggressively going after 12 Toronto-based publishing houses, with sales growth to $2M and projections to double sales and add Toronto sales office in 1992.

Edwards Brothers Inc. — Ann Arbor, MI   *1977–1985*

Northeast Regional Sales Manager — New York who realigned and reorganized the northeast sales department, retraining sales team, achieving Sales-By-Objective atmosphere and solid sales results. Increased region's sales by 20% in first year as manager. Established target goals for individuals and the department, including overall performance and new account development — targeting professional journal accounts and existing account growth.

Originally hired as *Sales Representative* and advanced through positions of *District Sales Manager* to *Regional Sales Manager* in 1983.

SUMMARY:

A consummate professional sales manager. Strong leadership skills. Great mentor for top performers; a team builder. Great market development skills. Strong technical knowledge.

BS, English and Journalism, Bowling Green State University, Ann Arbor, MI, 1975.

Example 7C

SCOTT BROOKS

Scott@aol.com

School Residence:	**Home Residence:**
224 Bracket Hall	**705 Fairview Ave.**
University of Colorado	**Monument, Colorado 80132**
College Phone: 303-786-4062	**Home: 719-481-3872**

WORK EXPERIENCE:

Hewlett Packard   *Summer 1999 and 2000*

* *Internship (Summer 2000)*

Worked in the Marketing division. Did research on competitor's products. Collected and entered data into a database.

* *Internship (Summer 1999)*

Worked in Test and Measurement division. Worked with little supervision testing for failures that caused software lockup of scope equipment.

EDUCATION:

Will graduate in top 10% of class with BS in Electrical Engineering from the University of Colorado, Boulder, CO in the Spring of 2001.

Elective Courses:
Magnetic Fields
Analog Design
C++ Programming

OTHER ACTIVITIES:

Captain—Men's Varsity Lacrosse, 1998 and 1999
Team Representative—For Student Athletic Advisory Committee

OTHER ACCOMPLISHMENT:

Attained Eagle Scout Rank in Boy Scouts of America (1995)

Example 7D

THOMAS D. FARMER

Thomas@aol.com

School Residence:
12 Fourth St., Apartment #7
Rochester, New York 14620
College Phone: (716) 786-4062

Home Residence:
705 Woodworth Ave.
Rochester, New York 14622
Home: (716)-252-1382

EDUCATION:

BS anticipated May 2003, Packaging Science-Management, Rochester Institute of Technology, Rochester, NY. G.P.A. 3.16 overall, field of study 3.41.

Elective Courses:
Packaging Materials, Engineering Design Graphics, Shock and Vibration, Medical Products Packaging.

WORK EXPERIENCE:

Procter and Gamble—Hunt Valley, MD   *Summer 2001 and 2002*

* *Internship/Cosmetics Division (Summer 2000)*

- Identified opportunities in mascara packaging and made recommendations based on patent research.
- Assisted in research of a new mascara package.

* *Internship/Pharmaceuticals Division (Summer 1999)*

- Became department expert on a new drop tester, and then trained engineers and technicians in the healthcare division.
- Assessed variation of an eye-drop bottle and provided data to show the bottle would meet specifications.
- Handled troubleshooting during experimental line trials.
- Researched all current blister leak-detection methods and recommended appropriate technology.
- Evaluated European Pharmacopoeia requirements to ensure the department did appropriate tests for global packages.

OTHER ACTIVITIES AND ACHIEVEMENTS:

Dean's List Fall 2000 and Spring, 2001
President of RIT Packaging Club, 2001-2002

Dual-Purpose Resume

Resumes that attempt to target two kinds of jobs are doomed to fail. Kevin Brown's resume, Example 7E on page 168 is just such a resume.

Kevin worked at a company that was facing major layoffs in the next several months. The company hired a firm to do resumes for its employees. Kevin was trying to decide if he could afford to change professions to a less stressful job, or if he needed to keep working as an engineer so he told the resume writer he wanted a resume that could be sent out for an engineering job or one as an apartment manager. The result was a resume that didn't present him well for either kind of work.

Many sacrifices were made in an attempt to create a dual-purpose resume. Kevin wanted the self-employed position as an apartment manager represented strongly on the resume. Doing this sacrificed room for his engineering job and the accomplishments he made there. In addition, Kevin wanted some jobs he had before he became an engineer so an employer for an apartment manager job would hopefully conclude he was versatile enough to accept other kinds of employment. Unfortunately, none of these jobs were represented with work dates, which diminishes the value of the information. Also missing is Kevin's college education. Perhaps the resume writer felt that because Kevin didn't receive a degree, the space was better used for other information. That was a poor choice. If you are working in any kind of technical field, always include college education on a resume, even if you don't have a degree.

Example F on page 170 shows how his resume for an engineering position needs to appear. Other resume style problems were also resolved. On the original resume, his job titles at Lockheed Martin Aerospace were listed as a group. In the redone versions, his accomplishments are put with each job title where they were made, giving an employer a better feel for Kevin's productivity in the workplace. His education is added, emphasizing studies that support his field of work. Information about his second job as an apartment manager is left off. This would do nothing to promote him as an engineer.

Example G on page 172 shows his resume for an apartment manager. For this resume, the Lockheed Martin Aerospace information is condensed. That allows for the apartment manager position to appear on the first page. With more room to concentrate on his apartment management skills, pertinent information can be added to his work history for that position. The second page shows the rest of his miscellaneous job history. Dates are now attached along with brief job descriptions. This shows he has abilities for jobs outside of the engineering field. In both overviews, the first statement talks about being cost-conscious. Kevin had a concern with the stigma of government projects and cost overruns. He wanted to communicate that he did his part to keep things in line with a budget. The Department of Defense Secret Clearance was kept on both resumes. This kind of clearance is associated with a high level of trust.

One resume will not serve for two entirely different jobs. Resumes need to be tailored to the job you are seeking; it isn't that difficult to generate a second resume.

Example 7E

Kevin R. Brown

740 Trumble Lane
Englewood, CO 80025

Home: 920-343-2573
Work: 920-871-5790

Kevin@aol.com

SUMMARY

- Mechanical/electrical interfacing and component/hardware layout, installation and inspection.
- Airborne and test cable design and manufacturing.
- Part specification and selection.
- Configuration management, inventory control, supervision and scheduling of manufacturing and production, inspection and support for launch site.
- Inspection and control of subcontractor's product and process.
- Sales and customer assistance, property management.
- Department of Defense (DOD) Secret Clearance.

PROFESSIONAL EXPERIENCE

LOCKHEED MARTIN AEROSPACE, Denver, CO   1984 – Present
Projects: Titan IV, Titan II, Athena, Space systems, and Emplacer
Senior Engineer, 2000 – Present
Engineer and Field Engineer, 1989 – 2000
Associate Engineer and Field Engineer, 1987 – 1989
Designer, 1984 – 1987

- Engineered cables from schematic to completion of hardware product for rockets, ground support, and test cables.
- Designed cable, box, and component mounting/installation with innovative new designs.
- Directed launch vehicle harness, hardware, and component installation. Evaluated and solved installation problems.
- Analyzed test and manufacturing errors and provided corrections and solutions.
- Inspected hardware, build logs, and product integrity reports for errors.
- Inspected vendor manufacturing facilities and processes to verify compliance of standards. Corrected production errors.
- Instructed, mentored, and supervised engineers and manufacturing technicians.
- Controlled manufacturing schedules and inventory control. Most projects were short design to launch "no slip schedules" and flexible to customer changes and fixed budgets.

SELF EMPLOYED, Lakewood, CO   1989 – Present
Part-time manage & maintain 11 units in Lakewood & Golden
Manager

- Manage and maintain rental property.
- Enforce rules and regulations.
- Schedule maintenance and renovation of buildings and individual units.
- Develop and maintain budget.
- Status resident satisfaction and provide solutions to keep turnovers at a minimum.
- Provide maximum rent and cost savings for the owner.

ADDITIONAL EXPERIENCE

FRED SCHMIDT APPLIANCE, Denver, CO
Sales Associate

- Assisted customers in the selection of appliances, stereos, and TV's.
- Provided follow up technical information to keep customer satisfied and a return client.

CENTENNIAL ENGINEERING, Arvada, CO
Designer

- Performed mechanical design and creation of drawings and parts list for concrete manufacturing plants and packaging facilities.

STERNS ROGERS, Denver, CO
Computer Operator

- Generated drawings using computer aided design for gas facilities, electrical facilities, and processing plants.

BUREAU OF RECLAMATION, Lakewood, CO
Technician

- Designed mechanical gates and spillways for hydroelectric doors.

TRAINING

Modern and Lean Manufacturing Training, plus 35 job related courses provided by employer.

AWARDS

Six letters of accomplishment and three performance awards for performing exceptional jobs.

COMPUTER SKILLS

- Wiring Design System (WDS)
- SDRC (Ideas) graphic software
- Mini Cads graphic software
- CADDS4X
- Wiring Design Checkout (EDE)
- Auto CAD graphic software
- Auto-trol graphic software

Example 7F

KEVIN R. BROWN

740 Trumble Lane
Englewood, CO 80025
Home: 920-343-2573
Work: 920-871-5790
Kevin@aol.com

OVERVIEW:

- Cost-conscious individual who is accustomed to meeting rigid schedules for project completion.
- Innovative designer of mechanical/electrical interfacing and component/hardware layout.
- Instructor and mentor.
- Skilled supervisor of projects from design through launch including inventory control, scheduling of manufacturing and production, and inspection and support for launch site.
- Department of Defense (DOD) clearance—Secret.

PROFESSIONAL EXPERIENCE:

Lockheed Martin Aerospace—Denver, CO   *1984–Present*

* *Senior Engineer Titan IV Project (2000–Present)*

- Support manufacturing during launch-vehicle cable installation and component installation.
- Troubleshoot test and manufacturing errors.
- Inspect hardware for engineering-requirement compliance and safety.
- Evaluate "build log" records, procedures, and product integrity reports for errors and hardware build issues.

* *Engineer and Field Engineer (1986–2000)*

Athena Launch Vehicle (1997–2000)

- Engineered and supported launch-vehicle cables from schematic to hardware completion, including test and installation.
- Supported and inspected vendor manufacturing facility and processes.
- Instructed, mentored, and supervised subordinate engineers and manufacturing technicians.
- Worked with short design-to-launch "no slip schedules" and a fixed budget while maintaining flexibility to adapt to customer changes.

Kevin R. Brown   *Page 2*

Space Systems (1996–1997)

- Engineered cables.
- Instructed, mentored, and supervised manufacturing technicians.
- Controlled inventory.
- Exceeded the schedules requirements by timely delivery of hardware.

Titan IV (1991–1996)

- Engineered cables, solved installation problems, and created innovative designs.
- Directed launch vehicle harness, hardware, and component installation.
- Inspected hardware, build logs/plans, and product integrity reports for errors.
- Instructed, mentored, and supervised associate engineers.

Titan II (1986–1991)

- Handled duties similar to those of the Titan IV project.
- Performed launch-site vehicle preflight inspection.

* *Associate Engineer and Field Engineer, Titan II (1986–1989)*
* *Designer, Emplacer Project (1984–1986)*

TRAINING:

Modern and Lean Manufacturing Training.

AWARDS:

Six letters of accomplishment and three performance awards for exceptional achievements.

COMPUTER SKILLS:

Wiring Design System (WDS)
Wiring Design Checkout (EDE)
SDRC (Ideas) graphic software
AutoCAD graphic software
Mini Cads graphic software
Auto-trol graphic software
CADDS4X

EDUCATION:

Classes toward an Electrical Engineering Degree, Denver College, 1974-1976

Example 7G

KEVIN R. BROWN

740 Trumble Lane
Englewood, CO 80025
Home: 920-343-2573
Work: 920-871-5790
Kevin@aol.com

OVERVIEW:

- Cost conscious individual who is accustomed to meeting rigid schedules for project completion.
- Sales and customer assistance experience.
- Property manager good at working as a liaison between owners and renters.
- Department of Defense (DOD) clearance—Secret.

PROFESSIONAL EXPERIENCE:

Lockheed Martin Aerospace—Denver, CO   *1984–Present*

* *Senior Engineer Titan IV Project (2000–Present)*

- Supervised launch project including budget management and hardware inspections.
- Met fast-paced schedules.
- Reviewed written operation procedures.
- Mentored associate engineers.

* *Engineer and Field Engineer (1989–2000)*
* *Associate Engineer (1986–1989)*
* *Designer (1984–1986)*

Apartment Manager—Lakewood, CO   *1989–Present*

* *Part-time*

- Part-time management and maintenance of 11 units in Lakewood and Golden.
- Enforce rules and regulations.
- Schedule maintenance and renovation of buildings and individual units.
- Develop and maintain budget.
- Work towards resident satisfaction and provide solutions to keep turnovers at a minimum.
- Provide maximum rent and cost savings for the owner.

Kevin R. Brown   *Page 2*

Fred Schmidt Appliance — Denver, CO   *1994-1995*

* *Sales Associate*

- Assisted customers in the selection of appliances, stereos, and TVs.
- Provided follow-up technical information to keep customers satisfied.

Centennial Engineering — Arvada, CO   *1981-1983*

* *Designer*

- Performed mechanical design and creation of drawings and parts lists.

Sterns Rogers — Denver, CO   *1979-1980*

* *Computer Operator*

- Generated drawings using computer-aided design for gas facilities, electrical facilities, and processing plants.

Bureau Of Reclamation — Lakewood, CO   *1974-1979*

* *Technician*

- Designed mechanical gates and spillways for hydroelectric dams.

TRAINING:

Modern and Lean Manufacturing Training.

AWARDS:

Six letters of accomplishment and three performance awards for exceptional achievements.

COMPUTER SKILLS:

Wiring Design System (WDS)   Mini Cads graphic software
Wiring Design Checkout (EDE)   Auto-trol graphic software
SDRC (Ideas) graphic software   CADDS4X
AutoCAD graphic software

EDUCATION:

Classes towards an Electrical Engineering Degree, Denver College, 1974-1976.

Non-Standard Resumes and Exceptions

Some companies or jobs request a resume, but the information they contain doesn't fit into the standard format. For the most part, unusual resumes need good organization and good presentation of material. The formatting tools in Chapter 4 work for these kinds of resumes.

Example 7H on page 175 is a resume for a seventeen-year-old who is applying for work at a veterinarian office as a kennel helper. Because of the kind of job and the applicant's age, club memberships, school affiliations, and hobbies and interests are included to help the employer get a sense of the applicant as a young person with varied interests.

Example 7I on page 176 is an example of a resume for a writer who was asked to send in a resume after she queried a dog magazine about writing articles. This type of resume is considered a functional resume.

Example 7H

SARA OLSEN

1705 Fairchild Avenue
Ingleside, Texas 78362
Home: 361-488-0156

WORK EXPERIENCE:

Burlages Ranch   *2/2000 to Present*

Care and cleaning of donkeys and horses Monday through Friday.

The Tidy Terrier   *Summer 2000*

Assisted in grooming of dogs.

Dog Training Instructions   *Summer 1999*

Went to people's homes and gave private lessons on techniques for training Jack Russell Terriers.

CLUB MEMBERSHIPS:

Member of Pikes Peak Obedience Club since 1998.
Member of Rocky Mountain Jack Russell Terrier Club since 1996.
Member of Jack Russell Terrier Club of America since 1996.

SCHOOL-AFFILIATED CLUBS:

Currently a member of WIP (Women in Power).
Member of Serteen for the school year 1999-2000.
Reader's and Writer's Quill 1998-2000.

HOBIES AND INTERESTS:

Horseback riding.
Showing Jack Russell Terriers at conformation, agility, and obedience.
Playing guitar.
Hiking.

Example 7I

JOAN ANDERSON

P.O. Box 245
Sante Fe, NM
Home: 505-488-6682
Fax: 505-488-0154
write@aol.com

WRITING EXPERIENCE:

Books

Authored *The New Owner's Guide to German Shepherds*

Dog Articles

* *Dog World Magazine*

"A Fight For Survival"

* *True Grit (Breed Magazine for Jack Russell Terriers)*

"Brucellosis, Know Your Enemy;" "Saving Our Breed;" "Fox vs. Terrier vs. Fox vs. Terrier"

* *New Dog Magazine*

"Mastering the Come Command"

* *Off-Lead Magazine*

"Buying Blindness," "Barking Control Devices"

Miscellaneous Magazines

New Shelter, Woman's World, Various Horse Magazines

EDUCATION:

BS, Biology with Studies in Writing, Metropolitan State College, 1978

CLUBS AND AFFILIATIONS:

Member of Dog Writers of America.
Professional Member of National Writers Association.

Chapter 8

Getting the Right Look on the Page

The Right Look

The right look on the page goes beyond the information contained, and at the same time is a reflection of the information contained.

The first page of a resume has a higher impact than any other page because it is the one most often viewed when the resume is sitting on a desk. At a glance, that first page can send your best information, or it can send a bad message. A less-favorable job listed at the bottom of the first page can have negative consequences. Bad page breaks can leave information stranded on the first or second page making the information hard to connect. Overall, at a glance, the first page needs to appear in good balance and look professional.

A Perfect Resume

Although a perfect resume isn't always achievable, there is a wish list for the appearance of a resume. The following is a wish list:

- The work history on the first page is the strongest representation of the candidate's most important skills and abilities.
- The overview is written as if the candidate knew the most important job qualifications the employer needed.
- The current job listed is pertinent to the job opening and tells about specific skills the employer needs for the job opening.
- The current company is composed of more than one job title because the candidate has worked his or her way up in the company.
- Each job title shows progression in job skills and accomplishments.
- On page two there are more companies with similar solid job history that support the candidate's strong points and consistency in achievement.
- The skills and education are easy to find and read on page two.
- There are no discrepancies in the employment record.

Making a strong presentation of the job history on the resume requires good organization and a font size large enough to be easy to read. A well-chosen font will maintain its integrity after a few faxings and will print out from an email intact. The white space on the ideal resume is used effectively and the resume is easy to skim for instant information.

Viewing Your "Look" on the Page

Often a good way to get an overall look at a resume is to view it under Print Preview in Microsoft Word. Spacing irregularities such as incorrect spacing between like and unlike material are easier to detect in Print Preview. Like material needs the same spacing and unlike material can have a different spacing to set it apart. The overall resume needs to look uncluttered and neat.

Improving First Page Impact

Sometimes by moving items from the first page to the second, or from the second page to the first, you can greatly improve your first page impact. You need to look at your resume and access if this can be done through the use of a few formatting techniques.

Moving a Job Position to the Second Page

Example 8A on page 179 is a resume for someone who wants to advance as a Sales Representative. Ted has not always been a Sales Representative and although he can't change his work history, leaving his earlier job as Headwaiter at the Outback Steak House on the first page works against his pursuit of his newer profession. He needs to move that information to the second page. With some formatting changes, he can move that job to the second page and still have a good presentation with his resume.

In Sample 8B on page 181, the waiter position is moved to the top of the second page. This was done by adding an extra paragraph return before the professional experience, and adding an additional paragraph return before the name. These help space the information on the page and result in the waiter position moving to the second page naturally. Just adding a page break would put the waiter position on the second page, but without the additional spacing, the information would look out of balance.

Do not change the chronological order of jobs to move around material in an attempt to improve the appearance of the first page. If you can't improve the resume through formatting, then you will have to leave less desirable information on the first page.

Example 8A

THEOBALD (TED) REVES

785 Onyx Avenue
Portales, New Mexico 88130
Home: 505-487-0359
Ted@Hotmail.com

OVERVIEW:

- Marketing and Sales with a management background.
- Strong office skills from human resource work through bookkeeping and accounting.

PROFESSIONAL EXPERIENCE:

Wonder Spring—Portales, NM   *1999–Present*

* *Sales Representative*

Sold water reservoirs and water purification systems in Santa Fe, Albuquerque, and the surrounding areas though cold calling and participation in trade shows. Started with a new territory and built the business to $100,000 in sales.

L&L Realty—McHenry, IL   *1997–1998*

* *Administrative Office Manager*

Managed the daily office operations of a four-star hotel while responsible for bookkeeping and accounting, payroll, processing applications, credit checks and employee benefits. Functioned as human resource administrator including the design of policies and procedures. Created, maintained, and enhanced operational filing systems, database, and contracts. Implemented marketing strategies. Designed and produced in-house graphics and communications. Coordinated and scheduled interior upgrades and maintenance for facility.

Senior Services Associates, Inc—Chicago, IL   *1996–1997*

* *Case Manager*

Conducted personal interviews in hospitals and in the community with nursing home applicants to determine eligibility, and to certify for Illinois Department on Aging (IDOA), including case management. Outreach involving public aid applications, and financial and personal assistance for seniors.

Outback Steakhouse—Denver, CO   *1994–1996*

* *Headwaiter*

Brighton Advertising Enterprises — Denver, CO   *1992–1994*

* *Art Director*

Developed advertising strategies and objectives for clients and handled client presentations, including advertising through design, copy writing, production and media placement of corporate identity pieces, brochures, print ads, manuals and newsletters. Handled client billing, job bidding, and estimates. Researched, selected, and installed software and hardware for Macintosh computers.

Ron Pine Advertising & Marketing — Denver, CO   *1991–1993*

* *Graphic Designer/Copywriter*

Responsible for design and copy writing of print advertising and brochures, including estimates for time and project quotes. Gave customer presentations. Allocated advertising budgets. Bought and scheduled media. Installed and troubleshot hardware and software for IBM computers.

Ethnic Magazine — Ames, IA   *1989–1991*

* *Advertising Manager*

Managed sales team. Conducted meetings with editors and sales staff of campus publications. Obtained advertising accounts and achieved goals. Established budgets and deadlines. Designed and produced local and national advertising.

Simpson Research — Des Moines, IA   *1988–1989*

* *Market Research Supervisor*

Trained and supervised team for market research.

EDUCATION:

BS, Journalism and Mass Communication with emphasis on Advertising Design, Iowa State University, Ames, IA, 1986.

Example 8B

THEOBALD (TED) REVES

785 Onyx Avenue
Portales, New Mexico 88130
Home: 505-487-0359
Ted@Hotmail.com

OVERVIEW:

- Marketing and Sales with a management background.
- Strong office skills from human resource work through bookkeeping and accounting.

PROFESSIONAL EXPERIENCE:

Wonder Spring — Portales, NM   *1999–Present*

* *Sales Representative*

Sold water reservoirs and water purification systems in Santa Fe, Albuquerque, and the surrounding areas though cold calling and participation in trade shows. Started with a new territory and built the business to $100,000 in sales.

L&L Realty — McHenry, IL   *1997–1998*

* *Administrative Office Manager*

Managed the daily office operations of a four-star hotel while responsible for bookkeeping and accounting, payroll, processing applications, credit checks and employee benefits. Functioned as human resource administrator including the design of policies and procedures. Created, maintained, and enhanced operational filing systems, database, and contracts. Implemented marketing strategies. Designed and produced in-house graphics and communications. Coordinated and scheduled interior upgrades and maintenance for facility.

Senior Services Associates, Inc — Chicago, IL   *1996–1997*

* *Case Manager*

Conducted personal interviews in hospitals and in the community with nursing home applicants to determine eligibility, and to certify for Illinois Department on Aging (IDOA), including case management. Outreach involving public aid applications, and financial and personal assistance for seniors.

Theobald (Ted) Reves *Page 2*

<u>*Outback Steakhouse—Denver, CO*</u>   <u>*1994-1996*</u>

* *Headwaiter*

<u>*Brighton Advertising Enterprises—Denver, CO*</u>   <u>*1992-1994*</u>

* *Art Director*

Developed advertising strategies and objectives for clients and handled client presentations, including advertising through design, copy writing, production and media placement of corporate identity pieces, brochures, print ads, manuals and newsletters. Handled client billing, job bidding, and estimates. Researched, selected, and installed software and hardware for Macintosh computers.

<u>*Ron Pine Advertising & Marketing—Denver, CO*</u>   <u>*1991-1993*</u>

* *Graphic Designer/Copywriter*

Responsible for design and copy writing of print advertising and brochures including estimates for time and project quotes. Gave customer presentations. Allocated advertising budgets. Bought and scheduled media. Installed and troubleshot hardware and software for IBM computers.

<u>*Ethnic Magazine—Ames, IA*</u>   <u>*1989-1991*</u>

* *Advertising Manager*

Managed sales team. Conducted meetings with editors and sales staff of campus publications. Obtained advertising accounts and achieved goals. Established budgets and deadlines. Designed and produced local and national advertising.

<u>*Simpson Research—Des Moines, IA*</u>   <u>*1988-1989*</u>

* *Market Research Supervisor*

Trained and supervised team for market research.

EDUCATION:

BS, Journalism and Mass Communication with emphasis on Advertising Design, Iowa State University, Ames, IA, 1986.

Stranding Information on a Page

Example 8C

In Sample 8C on page 184, Cynthia has stranded her last line of her work information as a Medical Assistant at Palm Springs Health Partners on the second page. This not only creates a poor first page presentation, but it forces an employer to waste time flipping between the first and the second page to connect the information. With a little reformatting, all the work history can be presented together. Although some work history must be split on two pages when dealing with only one or two lines, typically formatting adjustments can better group the information. She also needs a header on her second page.

Example 8D

Sample 8D on page 186, Ruth's resume, shows another kind of bad page break. As discussed in the previous example, the work information about each company needs to be contained in unbroken units. For Ruth's resume, the fix is as simple as adding a page break before Sam's Layout and Design. She also needs a header on her second page.

Example 8E

Sample 8E on page 188 covers a little more than one page. With a little formatting, this resume can appear on a single page. Removing space was as simple as removing extra paragraph spacing before Professional Experience and before Computer Skills. The results are seen in sample 8F on page 190.

Inserting a Page Break

When your resume needs to have information grouped differently on the page, the computer automatically does insert a page break as follows:

Insert>Break
Under *Break Types,* select **Page Break**.
Click OK.

After inserting a page break, make sure that the information on each page is distributed aesthetically. Don't have too much white space at the bottom of the first page as a result of adding a page break. Add any needed spacing between groups of material to better distribute the white space.

Checklist for Bad Page Breaks

- Bad breaks include the company and/or job title on one page and the work description and accomplishments on the next.
- All but one line of the work description and accomplishments on the first page.
- Sometimes it is a matter of information balancing. Too little information belonging to a heading on one page and the bulk on the next.

Example 8C

CYNTHIA R. STORER

7766 Crown Ave
Highlands, California 92346
Home: (408) 526-3675
Cindy@Yahoo.com

OVERVIEW:

- Solid client and candidate skills.
- Strong sales ability.
- Customer service and ability to development professional relationships with both clients and candidates.
- Talented at matching qualified candidates with the requirements of our clients.

PROFESSIONAL EXPERIENCE:

Global Staffing—Highlands, CA   *1996–Present*

* *Branch Manager (1997–Present)*

   - Acquired twenty-five new clients for business through cold calling.
   - Staffed both new and existing accounts.
   - Screened and interviewed candidates for placements.
   - Helped groom candidates for positions.
   - Oversaw training of office personnel and sales staff.
   - Conflict analysis and resolution.
   - Cost estimation.

* *Account Executive (1996–1997)*

   - Acquired new clients for the business through solicitations using mail, phone, and company visits.
   - Traveled throughout San Francisco and surrounding cities.
   - Developed new marketing ideas and strategies.
   - Provided strong customer service skills.

Palm Springs Health Partners, Palm Springs, CA   *1992–1995*

* *Medical Assistant*

   - Scheduled appointments, x-rays, and MRIs.
   - Charted patient history, vital statistics, and lab tests.
   - Called in prescriptions to pharmacies; gave injections and venipuncture.

- Maintained good patient relations.

<u>*US Navy — Norfolk, VA*</u>   <u>*1986–1990*</u>

* *Electronic Calibration Technician*

- Worked in electronic calibration lab in a job that required accuracy, precision and organizational skills.
- Inventoried supplies and did computerized tracking of shipments.
- Taught CPR as a certified instructor.

<u>EDUCATION:</u>

AA, Medical Office Assistant, Kee Business College, Norfolk, VA, 1992

<u>COURSES:</u>

Advanced Electronic Measurements Calibration Course, USA Military, 1987
Electronics and Electricity Course, Navy, 1986

<u>*COMPUTER SKILLS:*</u>

MS Word
Word Perfect
Microsoft Windows 2000

Example 8D

RUTH MORRELL

11775 Lavinia Lane
Newtown, Connecticut 06470
Home: (203) 280-8064
Connie@aol.com

OVERVIEW:

- Looking to reenter the publishing industry. Have been continually honing skills, and have consistently produced a newsletter for a dog club for the last three years.
- Strong management skills as a business manager.
- Good people skills and effective customer service techniques.

PROFESSIONAL EXPERIENCE:

The House Cleaner—Newtown, CT   *2002–Present*

* *Assistant Manager*

- Schedule workers for house cleaning.
- Manage employee problems.
- Total financial accounting responsibility.
- Complete charge of business when manager out of town.

Joseph and Son's, Inc.—Newtown, CT   *1999–2002*

* *Publications Director*

- Editing, proofing, and all duties of designing and prepress preparation for several association newsletters.
- Handled metered mailings.
- Made sure all deadlines were met.

A Dog's World—Newtown, CT   *1995–1999*

* *Publications Director*

- Produced a variety of dog breed magazines on monthly schedules.
- Responsible for selection of material that went into each publication.
- Worked with little supervision.

Sam's Layout and Design—New Town, CT   *1993–1994*

* *Typesetting and Production Artist*

- Worked for national publications and for local sales company, that produced outdoor books & maps.
- Created computer-generated maps for a series of trail guidebooks.
- Set up ads for *The Star* (National Mercedes Benz publication).
- Provided required attention to detail and accuracy.

All Seasons Enterprises and Remuda Manufacturing — New York, NY   *1985–1993*

* *Co-Owner and Business Manager*

- Designed all the printed marketing and business identity materials, including ads in national magazines.
- Responsible for all the operations of a small business, including training and scheduling employees, and doing payroll.

OTHER APPLICABLE EXPERIENCE:

Mac Temps — Fill in Work in between permanent jobs, including prepress work.
Freelance publishing — typesetting, layout, transcribing interviews, proofreading, and editing in between permanent jobs.
Publisher of Jack Russell Terrier Newsletter.

COURSES:

Various Classes in Computer aided Typography, QuarkXPress, Adobe Illustrator, Adobe Photoshop.
Various Drawing and Fine Art classes, Rocky Mountain College Of Art And Design.
Aldus PageMaker and Typing classes, Pickens Technical School.
Power Macintosh G3, HP Scan Jet IIp and HP LaserJet III, as ongoing study to improve and update my skills in QuarkXPress, Adobe Illustrator, and Adobe Photoshop. Read books on related subjects.

Example 8E

KIM LEAK

PO Box 814
Dallas, Texas
Home: 214-748-8523
Kim@juno.com

OVERVIEW:

- Talented office manager with bookkeeping skills.
- Strong customer service abilities.
- Public relations experience.

PROFESSIONAL EXPERIENCE:

Skin Savvy Laser Clinic—Dallas, TX   *1999–Present*

* *Office Manager*

- Operate four-line phone system and schedule customers.
- Order supplies and product. Handle inventory.
- Customer service.
- Perform basic accounting, including accounts payable and accounts receivable.

Whispering Winds Assisted Living—Dallas, TX   *1996–1999*

* *Facilities Manager, Head CNA*

- Handled pubic relations meetings for the medical community.
- Directed activities.
- Dietary management.
- Ordered supplies.
- Reception and assisting clients.

GT Global Staffing—Dallas, TX   *1990–1996*

* *Receptionist/Recruiter*

- Interviewing and reference checks.
- Operated three-line reception.
- Performed clerical work, including filing, faxing, and organizing.

COMPUTER SKILLS:

Microsoft Word
Windows 2000

Example 8F

KIM LEAK

PO Box 814
Dallas, Texas
Home: 214-748-8523
Kim@juno.com

OVERVIEW:

- Talented office manager with bookkeeping skills.
- Strong customer service abilities.
- Public relations experience.

PROFESSIONAL EXPERIENCE:

Skin Savvy Laser Clinic—Dallas, TX   *1999–Present*

* *Office Manager*

- Operate four-line phone system and schedule customers.
- Order supplies and product. Handle inventory.
- Customer service.
- Perform basic accounting, including accounts payable and accounts receivable.

Whispering Winds Assisted Living—Dallas, TX   *1996–1999*

* *Facilities Manager, Head CNA*

- Handled pubic relations meetings for the medical community.
- Directed activities.
- Dietary management.
- Ordered supplies.
- Reception and assisting clients.

GT Global Staffing—Dallas, TX   *1990–1996*

* *Receptionist/Recruiter*

- Interviewing and reference checks.
- Operated three-line reception.
- Performed clerical work, including filing, faxing, and organizing.

COMPUTER SKILLS:

Microsoft Word
Windows 2000

Getting More on the Page

Using Smaller Font

Sometimes you need to get just a little more of the resume contents on each page to either contain your resume on two pages or to get the right look on the first page. Changing the font size is one way to do this. If you're using Book Antiqua, 12 points, you can change the font to 11.5 points. This is the minimum size that maintains faxability. If more reductions are needed, use other techniques.

> When you change font size, you need to make sure you apply the new font size to the entire resume. Before you change the font size, first select the entire resume. The quick way to do this is to use the Select All function. From the menu bar select Edit>Select All. This selects the entire contents of the resume. Now when you change the font size under *Format>Font* on the Menu bar, it will apply to the entire resume.

Removing Space After Tags

To get more of the resume contents on a page, you can remove some of the space after the Tags. Those tags include: Name, Address, Header, Company Name, and Title. For example, you can select the text tag *Name.*
To remove spacing after that tag, first select a line of text with the Name tag applied (this should be your name typed on the resume).
On the menu bar, select *Format>Paragraph*
In the *Spacing/After* box you will see *10 points.* You can lower that spacing to **8 points.**
Click on OK.

The following tags can be reduced if necessary.
Name changed from *10 points* to **8 points.**
Address changed from *22 points* to **18 points.**
Heading changed from *10 points* to **8 points.**
Company changed from *10 points* to **8 points.**
Job Title changed from *10 points* to **8 points.**

> With each adjustment, check the look on the page under Print Preview and make sure things still look in balance. You may need to redo some of the spacing for different tags to secure a balanced appearance.

Applying the Spacing Changes to the Entire Resume

The change you made will only affect the line that is highlighted. To transfer the change to all the *Tags* used in the resume, you need to do the following:

Highlight the tag line you just changed. For this example, let's say you just changed the spacing after the Job Title tag.

From the formatting tool bar, click on the *Style* box down arrow. In the example below, the style box has the word *title* in it. From the drop down menu, click on the word title, even though it is already highlighted.

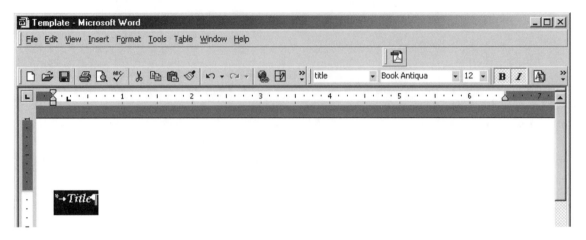

The dialog box you see below should appear. Choose "Update the style to reflect recent changes?" Click on OK. This will change the spacing throughout the resume.

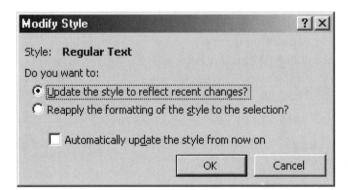

Adjusting Margins

To get more of the resume contents on a page, the margins on the resume can be reduced from 1 inch all around to 0.8 inch on the sides. Sometimes this can be done stepwise by first adjusting the sides, and then if more space is needed, adjusting the top and bottom. To change the page margins, from the menu bar, select *File>Page Setup*. The margins are found under the *Margins* tab.

Be aware that using a margin less than 0.8 inch risks having part of the resume lost in the faxing process, or part printed on a separate page after emailing.

Dealing With Less on a Page

- Change the margins for the page layout to 1.25 inches all around.
- Add a paragraph space before the name.
- Add an extra paragraph space between company units (company name, title, job description and accomplishments).
- Add an extra paragraph space after the contact information.
- Use two paragraph marks between categories like Education and Skills, and to separate the work history from the categories.
- Check the final look under page preview and make adjustments to anything that looks poorly spaced.

When adding paragraph spaces, be sure to use the Normal tag for the paragraph insertion. This will make the amount of spacing added more consistent than if you mix the paragraph tags.

The Final Analysis

After you've rearranged your resume and made your spacing adjustments, look under Print Preview. Do the items look balanced on the page? Are like items spaced so they look as if they belong together? Is the spacing between unlike material different from the spacing between like material? If the resume looks well presented and balanced under Print Preview, you are ready to review it in a hard copy.

Chapter 9

More Help on Rewriting

> This chapter provides more advice on writing different parts of the resume and some techniques for better writing.

Eliminate Redundant Words

Example

Raw material sent in as a finished resume:

* *Manager—Production Purchasing (January 1999–Present)*

Currently responsible for managing day-to-day production of targeted and repeat-order direct-mail campaigns as well as the Acknowledgement and Billing Program (including fulfillment/renewals), amounting to a budget of well over $20 Million dollars annually. Report directly to Director of Production/Purchasing and supervise three direct reports in the group. Prepare mailing budgets, cost analysis, and production schedules. Hold meetings as needed. Perform employee evaluations and reviews as scheduled for the staff.

> **Below, the problem words from the job information are bolded.**
> **Currently** responsible for managing day-to-day production of targeted and repeat-order direct-mail campaigns as well as the **Acknowledgement and Billing Program** (including fulfillment/renewals), amounting to a budget of well over $20 Million **dollars** annually. **Report directly to Director of Production/Purchasing** and supervise three direct reports in the group. Prepare mailing budgets, cost analysis, production schedules, and hold meetings as needed. Perform employee evaluations and reviews as scheduled for the staff.

Clean Things Up

- Eliminate *currently* because that is implied by the work date above, which states present.
- Eliminate the name of programs like *Acknowledgement and Billing Program* because in this case, they are unique to the specific company and not common terms used in the industry. That makes them useless to another employer.
- Eliminate the word *dollars*. That is already stated by the dollar sign.

- Eliminate Report directly to Director of Production/Purchasing. Seldom is there any value outside of your company to state who you reported to because outside of your company, few people will know the true significance of that person.

Example

Raw material sent in as a finished resume:

* *Manager — Production Purchasing (January 1999–Present)*

- Generate over $20 million annually through management of the day-to-day production of targeted and repeat-order, direct-mail campaigns, fulfillment, and renewals.
- Prepare mailing budgets, cost analyses, and production schedules, as well as conduct meetings.
- Supervise three direct reports, including evaluations and reviews.

Eliminate Vague Words

Certain phrases, statements and words on resumes add no value to the candidate or to the additional information for the employer. These need to be eliminated. They include:

- Words such as et cetera have no value in a resume.
- Ending a statement with "as needed" doesn't add information. The employer typically won't assume you only did the task when it *wasn't* needed. They figure you did it *as needed*.
- The word *currently* isn't needed when stating a task for a job you presently hold.
- Leave out statements like "Performed evaluations and reviews as scheduled." It is better to say "performed evaluations and reviews monthly." If the work was not done on a schedule, often including a time element isn't necessary. "Performed evaluations and reviews." is enough.
- Either you worked on the project or you didn't. Don't be vague by saying you assisted with, or worked as part of a team. Statements like "worked as part of a team" or "helped research" takes up too much room and sounds weak. Either you did enough work on the project to claim significant credit or you weren't a real contributor. If you were a real contributor, state something like "Researched new techniques for two-fold manufacturing process resulting in conversion of half the manufacturing equipment."

Eliminate Qualifiers

Stay away from words like *approximately*, *mostly*, *generally* and other qualifying words. Scrutinize all words ending in *ly*. These adverbs often can be cut or the text rewritten with more powerful verbs and specific details that qualify your success. Example: "Costs were lowered dramatically" is better stated by "Generated a savings of $250,000 on the first printing." Another example: "Worked closely with marketing to produce a new presentation." The word closely doesn't tell how close you really were. It is better to state: "Worked with marketing department to develop a new presentation."

Don't State Incomplete Information

"Presented monthly financial report to plant and senior management." is incomplete information. The statement doesn't tell the results or why the action was significant or why it was important to present the report to the plant and senior management. If the monthly financial reports are a typical part of the job, state it as follows: "Generated monthly financial report."

State Actions and Results

"Directed the startup of two major equipment installations (NP500 Insert System and the Bushman Delivery system).

However, don't state actions that result in a negative message. "Researched new techniques for two-fold manufacturing process that resulted in abandonment of that idea." If you feel it is necessary to make a statement about your research, make the results more positive: "Evaluated two-fold manufacturing process."

Work to eliminate phrases such as *Responsible for* and *duties included*. Use action verbs instead.

Example

Responsible for all the operations of a small business.
Changed to
Managed all the operations of a small business.

Responsible for securing a large, variable digital color program that required major corporate capital expenditure.
Changed to
Secured a large, variable digital color program that required major corporate capital expenditure.

Duties included the day-to-day management of the accounting department.
Changed to
Managed the accounting department.

Exposure to many large-volume mailings requiring planning and monitoring of production.
Changed to
Assisted in planning and monitoring production for large-volume mailings.

Although the ideal is to scrutinize certain phrases such as *responsible for*, they don't all need to be eliminated.

Writing Better Work Histories

In the following example, a candidate wrote a description of his sales manager position. The second example illustrates another way of presenting the same information. Notice how much more intriguing the candidate sounds with the powerful job description.

Example

Original:

* *Regional Sales Manager*

- Managed seven sales executives in a six-state region within the $1 Billion-plus Corporate Sales Unit.
- Grew region from $80M to $145M in two years.
- Highest percentage top-line AND bottom line growth rate for both years in entire Corporate Sales.
- National sponsor/director for sales training and performance leadership. Heavily involved in corporate-wide strategic planning process as well as major capital appropriation projects both years.

Better:

* *Regional Sales Manager*

Regional Sales Manager for six northwest states. Maintained senior sales representative responsibilities while assuming administration, training, hiring, forecasting, budgeting, and performance objectives for the region.

- Achieved highest sales revenue growth rate in the company all three years and highest gross profit growth rate.
- Evolved business base from only 24% of work secured on a term contract to over 85% in two years, creating a gain in gross revenue of $65M.
- Trained two sales representatives who went on to win Sales Rookie of the Year for RRD.
- Tracked record of personnel development, high-performance culture generation, and results both personally and with employees.

Write Good Job Descriptions

Use details in job descriptions to be specific, but don't be overly specific. Too generalized also isn't good. Find a nice balance.

Example

* *Vice President of Operations*

Responsible for manufacturing at the Philadelphia facility and others. Oversaw manufacturing, engineering, human resources, warehousing, and logistics.

Better

* Vice President of Operations*

Responsible for all North American flexible packaging businesses with five business-unit leaders in three locations and over $70M in revenue. Oversaw manufacturing, engineering, new product development, customer service, and marketing, supporting a centralized sales force. One business was non-union; the other was Teamsters.

> In the original statement, the word *and others* has no significance to anyone other than the person who stated it. The second description paints a clearer picture. Often, you need to look at what is on your resume and see what kind of a picture it paints for others. Too much detail and it gets skimmed over. Too vague and it looses its significance altogether.

Scrutinize Company Information

> Similarities in companies need to be pointed out. If you are working for a Fortune 500 company and you are applying to a similar company, make sure that information is stated under your current job. Size similarities need to be stated when they are an advantage. For example, if the company has a similar annual sales volume or production volume, state those facts. If similarities that exist are not an advantage (for example, if you are currently working for a large company and wish to be employed at a small one), leave off that detail. In the examples below, the company Prairie Manufacturing can use more identification.

Example

Original

Prairie Manufacturing—Dayton, OH   **_1996–Present_**

> The company name doesn't tell what the company manufactures.

Better

Prairie Manufacturing—Dayton, OH   **_1996–Present_**
The third-largest corrugated-box manufacturer in the United States.

Or

Prairie Manufacturing—Dayton, OH   **_1996–Present_**
A corrugated-box manufacturer.

> When you are choosing to use extra information about a company, do so with discretion. The more important the company information is to the job that the resume is targeting, the more likely additional information will be offered. Don't include descriptive information about every company. Include it only when there is relevance to the job this resume is targeting. The information in a resume is all a matter of balance with who you are, what you want to say about yourself, and what the employer needs to know in order to determine whether or not to interview you.

Tightening Up and Correcting Sentences

Company Names That are too Long

If the company name, address, and work dates run over two lines, try to reduce the information to fit onto one line. Use some of the following techniques:

- Put division information on lower line.
- Use abbreviations for the words *company*, *incorporated*, or similar status information.
- Eliminate any excess company nomenclature. Use what is important for identifying the company by name, but no extra information if it doesn't have relevance to a resume reader in determining your qualifications. For instance, often you can drop a division name.

Sentence Structure

In General

- Avoid long compound sentences.
- Make sure your sentences aren't so fragmented they don't have value and clarity.

Use Parallel Sentence Structure

- Parts of speech need to be parallel.
- Usually a signal of problems in parallel structure is a mixture of "ing" and "ed" in the same sentence.

Example
Not parallel:

- Increas<u>ed</u> efficiency and contro<u>lling</u> costs.

Parallel:

- Increas<u>ed</u> efficiency and controll<u>ed</u> costs.

or

- Increas<u>ing</u> efficiency and controll<u>ing</u> costs.

Write Actively

- Start sentence fragments with action verbs.
- Vary the beginnings of the sentences.

Stating Accomplishments

- Put them in bullets.
- Don't use the word *accomplishment* to announce them.

Arrangement of the Bulleted Material

- Put the most relevant first.
- Group like material together.

Paragraphing Job Duties

Sometimes bullets are the best way to show the job duties. At other times, job duties appear best in a paragraph followed by accomplishments for that job in bullets below the paragraph.

In general, when duties are distinguishably different from accomplishments, put them in a paragraph and use bullets afterwards for the accomplishments. Only use a paragraph for job duties when it gives significance and/or power to the resume. If the job duties are understood, don't list them. If they are a repeat of the previous job listed on the resume, don't repeat them but make a reference to their listing elsewhere. If job duties and accomplishments aren't easily separated, bullet them all.

Don't Use Lists in an Overview

Example
Not This Way:

Customer Service Engineer with more than 15 years of experience in the telecommunications and high-tech industries. Major skills include, technical training, service documentation development/writing, and in-depth troubleshooting. Additional skills include:

Management
Project Management
Team Lead
Seminars/Training
Entrepreneurial Experience
Field Technical Support
Computer Repair
Time Management
Mentoring

One- or two-word lists do not convey enough information. For instance, in this example management and project management are both listed. What is the difference? Is Team Lead old news that his person has grown past, or is it the level this person is really at now. What went on with the seminars and training? Did this person attend them or conduct them? We may assume the person conducted them, but did he or she write them or just present them? If the employer cares about seminars and training, present specific information in the context of the overview, not in another list. What is this entrepreneurial experience? Is this person going to be nagging about new ideas that don't pan out? Did this person actually make a contribution with an entrepreneurial idea? What kind of field support? Computer repair may or may not matter to the employer, but this is too vague to determine. Time management doesn't say anything. Mentoring can be strengthened with a little more expansion, and needs to appear in the body of the overview, not in a list.

Example
This Way:

- Project Lead on three projects that produced instruments that topped sales expectations by 12%.
- Conducted seminars and training on two new products in the United States and Europe, adding to the gross 25% sales of the products.
- Fielded questions from customers on product applications. Resolved function issues and reported problems for quick resolutions.
- Mentored engineers for seminar and training to take product to Asian markets.
- In-depth hardware troubleshooting skills.
- Wrote and developed service manuals.

Can more be said? Can different information be presented in this overview? Yes, depending upon the position this resume is targeting. Making the effort to choose the most important information and elaborate on it give what you say more relevance. Often more than one resume is needed when sending out to several potential employers. Taking the time to tweak the overview for each employer can make the difference between the rejection pile and the one where they call you for interviews.

Chapter 10

Edits and Final Touches

Before you print the final resume, there are some final edits that need to be made. This chapter offers information on common grammar errors seen on resumes, as well as the checklist to use before you send out your resume. A final copy of a resume needs to be printed on white (not bright white) or slightly off-white, twenty-four pound paper, and needs to be clean and error-free. Don't use colored or fancy paper for a resume.

Grammar and Style Rules

Books are written on grammar and style, and style rules vary with different publications. For resumes, a good reference book for grammar and style is *The Gregg Reference Manual* by William A. Sabin. This is a well-accepted stylebook for businesses. The following is not intended to be a complete guide for grammar and style rules, but represents some of the common issues encountered on resumes.

Periods

States are abbreviated either Tx. (with the period) or TX (without the period). A common mistake is for people to use two capital letters with periods. Never use the period when using both capital letters. The preferred form is to use both capital letters.

Even when using incomplete sentences, use a period. With lists, you can omit a period, but bulleted summaries are usually more than a list and need a period. Use a period at the end of any statements.

Don't use periods after Roman numerals. For example, *Volume III* or *John Smith III*.

Use a period inside parentheses when the sentence contained inside those parentheses is complete. Use the period outside the parentheses when the information isn't a complete sentence. Example:

The second installation of the material that I personally managed was a total success.

The operation succeeded without any problems, (at least as long as I was the supervisor).

In general, using parentheses in a resume tends to be interruptive. If possible, rewrite the information to exclude the parentheses.

Commas

Serial Commas

When stating a series, use the comma to separate the last item in the series from the word *and*.

Example

Products sold included oranges, apples, and grapefruit.

This style makes it clearer that there are three products. Without the comma before the last item in a series, the meaning can become confusing so always use a serial comma, even when you think there is no potential for confusion.

Interrupting Elements

Commas are used to set off interrupting elements in sentences and afterthoughts. This style of writing usually doesn't work as well in a tightly structured resume because it is too interruptive. Avoid interruptive elements.

Use with Introductory Clauses

Although a comma is used correctly with sentence interruptions and afterthoughts like *however*, *therefore*, and *to be honest*, according to most authorities, resumes are better rewritten to exclude those words and phrases.

Use with Contrasting Expressions

These expressions include *but*, *not*, or *rather than*.

Example

Carol, rather than Sara, was chosen for the position.

Commas in Dates

Use commas to set off the year when it follows the month and day. Omit the comma when only the month and year are used.

Example

On September 15, 2003, I will be available for a new position.
In May 2002, I sold my business and started consulting.

Commas with the Status of a Business

Don't use commas to set off *LLC, Inc.* or similar expressions in the company name unless you know that particular company does it that way. If in doubt, leave it out.

With Cities and States

Use a comma to separate a city and state. Use a comma for Washington, D.C.

Numbers

Dollars are best presented numerically. For example, $25 is quick and easy to read on a resume. The spelled out form is not. There is no space between the dollar sign and the numbers.

Avoid spelling out large numbers. Twenty-five million dollars isn't as easy to understand as the number $25,000,000. The best way to represent numbers is to abbreviate them even more, which makes them easier to read and grasp at a glance. Either $25 million or $25M are acceptable abbreviations.

Shorten longer figures and round off numbers. Never put a period and two zeros on any figure.

Example

Not: $25,000.00. *Instead* write $25,000.

Never repeat the word *dollars* when the dollar sign is used.

Example

Not: $500,000 dollars. *Instead* $ is preferred for readability.

In General
- Be consistent with whatever style you choose for representing your numbers. Don't use $25M one time and $25,000,000 elsewhere in the resume.
- It is not necessary to spell out a number and then put the numeral equivalent in parentheses, such as *one-hundred (100)*. Although this style is seen on some legal documents, it doesn't belong on a resume.
- The basic rule for presenting numbers: Above ten, use Arabic numerals, one to ten, spell out, even if it creates a mixture of forms in the same sentence. For example: Increased sales territory from nine states to 12 in four months.

> Although the guidelines state to use Arabic numerals above ten, and spell out digits below ten, if the final product reads more quickly and clearly when you keep the numbers in one consistent form, such as the Arabic numeral, choose what is the easiest to read over the style rule.

Percentages.

Similar rules apply to percentages apply to dollars. Don't put the percent sign and then state *percent*.

Example

Not: 30% percent. *Instead,* 30% or 30 percent. Preferably use the word percent if you are spelling out the amount (usually in smaller numbers under ten) such as when stating *five percent*.

Although the general rule is to spell out numbers under ten, sometimes it is better to bend the rule to keep the information consistent and more easily read. For example, it is better to use *5%, 17%* and *40%* instead of *five percent, 17%* and *40%*.

Colon

In general, use a colon when a list is going to follow.

Example

My job consisted of the following duties:
Key words that introduce a list include *the following, as follows, thus,* and *these*.
I performed the following duties:

Semicolon

Use a semicolon to separate independent clauses when the conjunction *and, but,* or *or* is omitted and the second clause doesn't explain the first.

Use a semicolon between two independent clauses that are separated by *however, furthermore, consequently, therefore, nevertheless, accordingly*. These words are best avoided on a resume, as are the use of semicolons. Generally it is better to create two sentences and begin the second with *however*. Doing this enhances readability.

Dashes

Don't put a space before or after any kind of dash. The word processing program is already coded to include the right amount of space.

The Em Dash

Use an em dash (or long dash) between text and in sentence interruptions (when using in place of commas to set off the text). Use this dash sparingly. If you find your work history containing a lot of em dashes, consider rewriting.

The em dash can be inserted by choosing Insert from the menu bar in Microsoft Word, choosing Symbol, and then selecting Special. Follow the directions in the dialog box that opens. The em dash also can be inserted by depressing the Alt and Ctrl key together and then using the dash on the numeric keypad on the right side of the keyboard.

The En Dash

Use an en dash (or medium dash) between dates of employment.

The en dash can be inserted from the menu by following the above for the em dash. To insert using the key board, depress the Ctrl key and then use the dash on the numeric keypad on the right side of the keyboard.

The Regular Dash or Hyphen

Use a regular dash or hyphen (the one on the row top of the typing section of the key board) when hyphenating words.

Use a hyphen for a compound number. Example: Twenty-two.

Use a hyphen for compound modifiers. Example: A well-known business for years. In general, don't use so many compound modifiers that the resume is littered with hyphens.

Don't use a hyphen when using compound words as verbs. When the words are used as nouns or adjectives, they often require hyphens. Sometimes they can be written as one word without a hyphen. Check in a standard dictionary to be sure that you are hyphenating words correctly. A good online resource is the Merriam-Webster Web site (www.M-W.com).

Use hyphenation when the title includes two functions such as *Owner-Manager*.

Slashes

You also can use slashes when the title includes two functions. Example: Owner/Manager.

Exclamation Points

Don't use them. They don't add excitement and emphasis to what you did, but they do make you look amateurish. They never belong on a resume.

Italics and Underlining

Use italics for titles of books, periodicals, movies, plays, and television and radio programs. These used to be underlined when people used typewriters. Now with word processors, it is easy to use italics and italics are preferred.

Parentheses

When parentheses enclose a complete sentence, put the period inside the parentheses. If the words inside the parentheses do not form a complete sentence, but simply end a sentence that began before the parentheses, place the period outside. In general, don't have a lot of text with parentheses in your resume.

Possessives

Adding an apostrophe or an apostrophe/*s* to a noun forms the possessive. The possessive expresses ownership. If the noun is plural, add only an apostrophe. If the noun is singular, add an apostrophe plus *s*.

Quotation Marks

Use quotation marks for coined words or business jargon that may not be familiar. Also, use quotation marks to add clarity to a sentence.

The Use of Personal Pronouns

Don't use *I* or *me* in the resume. Rewrite to eliminate any personal references.

Tense

If the job is current, use present tense. If the job is not current, use past tense. If you can't accurately use present tense, use past tense for the entire resume. Never use the present tense for previous jobs in the work history.

Acronyms

An acronym is a shortened form derived from the initial letters of the words that make up the complete form. For example, *ZIP* is an acronym for *Zone Improvement Plan*. Most people know this term so putting an explanation is not necessary.

The rules for using an acronym in resumes include the following:
- Use all capitals without any periods.
- Don't use the acronym if few people will recognize it. Type out the entire name. For example, "Moved up from WATS to Sales Representative in five months." is better written "Moved up from Wide-Area Telecommunications Service Technician to Sales Representative in five months." If you need to use the acronym more than once, introduce it with an explanation and then use the abbreviated form only.
  For example: *Moved up from WATS (Wide-Area Telecommunications Service) to Sales Representative in five months.*
  Use this form when you plan to use the WATS acronym later in the resume, or when you feel strongly that some resume readers will understand what WATS is while others will understand Wide-Area Telecommunications Service.
- If the acronym is more likely to be recognized than the actual name, use the more recognizable form.
- Use a common acronym like ZIP without explanation when most people understand it.
- In general, don't waste words on explaining acronyms unless you must do so for the sake of clarity. Write only what is necessary to communicate information to the reader.

Spacing With Word Processors

Today's word processing programs are created to put in the correct spacing after punctuation and before and after dashes and slashes. With the exception of using Courier, don't enter the same spacing you would if you were using a typewriter. Some guidelines are listed below when using word processing programs.

Dashes
No spaces before or after.

Periods:
One space after the end of a sentence.
No spaces after initials.

Diagonals or Slashes
No spaces before or after.

Colons
Only one space after a colon.

Commas and semicolons
Only one space after either.

Questions
Only one space after.

Capitalization

Capitalize a proper noun. Some job titles are used as proper nouns, and at that time, they are capitalized. Some department names fall under the same rule. However, don't capitalize for emphasis. One of the few exceptions to this rule is with job titles. If you choose to capitalize job titles, do so with discretion.

If the name of a department is used as a proper noun, capitalize it. If the name of the department is not used as a proper noun, don't capitalize it. If the name is a department description, don't capitalize it.

Contractions

In more formal writing, it is best to avoid the use of contractions. However, if not using a contraction makes the resume read unsmoothly, use the contraction.

Degrees

When stating a degree such as BS degree, the word degree is redundant.

Although technically a degree is accompanied by periods such as B.S., it is acceptable to just use the initials without periods, such as *BS*.

Only the year is necessary for a graduation date. Don't include the month. If no degree was obtained, include the range of years attended.

PitFalls and Nevers

Pitfalls to Avoid In Your Resume

1. Job Duties
Don't create a grocery list of job duties.
Some resumes merely list job duties and give one-liners for responsibilities. This may jog the resume creator's memory about what went on in the job, but does little for the employer.

Don't create a boring job duty section.
Only put in what is needed for communication about the job. This area is used to inform the employer about what you can do without getting into details about the little things. Think in broad strokes.

Don't forget your contributions.
Go beyond showing what was required; tell how you made a difference at each company. When possible, provide specific examples.

2. Objective Statements
Don't use objective statements.
Such statements waste space on a resume and are seldom read.
Few objective statements are original. A lot of them say something like: "Seeking a challenging position that will enable me to contribute to organizational goals while offering an opportunity for growth and advancement." Not only is this overused, but look at what it is really saying. It basically says, "I want a good job that I will like." The employer certainly hopes this is true of anyone hired. The interview is where the employer gets a feel for your long-term desires and motivations for taking the job.

3. Don't Make a Resume Too Long or Too Short
For most people, two pages is the right length for a resume.
Some people will find their information fitting onto one or one-and-a-half pages. If your resume seems short, look over the contents and make sure statements are not too brief. On the other hand, don't let a resume become too long. If you are going into three pages with the work history, you need to do some serious editing. Don't assume that anyone is willing to read a lot of material just because you wrote it.

A checklist for too short: Make sure you haven't left out any impressive achievements. Make sure you aren't using one word when more are needed for a clear understanding.

A checklist for too long: Make sure you aren't rambling or being redundant. Similar work experiences can be more detailed in recent positions and summarized in earlier positions.

Remember, what you write in the resume is designed to get you an interview, not to detail every little thing you did on the job. Work to make every word help sell you.

4. Don't Use I or Me.
A resume is a business communication. Leave out personal pronouns.

5. Leave Out Personal Information
Don't state your interests.
The exception is if your personal interests have a direct impact on the job. If you are an avid outdoor hunter and you are applying to a sporting goods shop, list that interest.

Don't give physical, ethnic, or any other personal information.
Don't state date of birth, marital status, height and weight, and never include a picture of yourself. If you are not a U.S. citizen, you can state that you have a Green Card. That relates directly to your ability to work. So does the mastery of a foreign language.

6. Never Use a Functional Resume
A true functional resume will not include work dates. Do not use this kind of resume when applying for a conventional job. If you need to emphasize items outside your work history, do so by using an extensive Overview to give yourself a strong profile. Although some of the work history may warrant only a brief statement about what was done in that position, a work history is needed on a resume, even if none of the work applies to the current position. A work history that doesn't apply to the field you apply for a job in can still tell a lot about you, such as how long you tend to stay at a job and if you tend to do more than the minimum requirements for the position.

7. Don't Reverse Chronological Employment History
You can list jobs and dates without detail if you need to include less recent experience near the end of the resume that fits the current job, but keep with the correct order of listing the most recent job first. Don't make an employer unravel a puzzle with your job history.

8. Don't Forget to Include Keywords
Some companies scan resumes into a database and use a program to categorize your skills. That program chooses keywords to classify you. Be sure you have the customary industry words in your resume at least once. A good way to help determine keywords is to read a job description on line or in the newspaper about the position you are applying for.

9. Leave Off the Statement: References Available
Employers already assume this. Also, never offer references without a request.

10. Don't Forget to Have a Friend Proofread the Resume

Typos are the kiss of death. It is always hard for the person who creates the resume to catch all of their mistakes. If you don't have someone to help proof your resume, allow a cooling off time before you try to proof it yourself. Some people find it helpful to read the material in reverse when looking for typos.

11. Don't Tempt the Resume Reader to Toss Your Resume

Here are some reasons resumes are tossed:

- Hard to read due to small font or poorly chosen font style.
- Not tailored to the target job.
- Poor organization.
- Work history presented in the wrong order.
- Work dates hard to find, company name hard to distinguish, title difficult to locate.
- A resume that is too short because it is incomplete.
- Grammar and typing errors.

Remember, some employers view the resume as an insight into the person—especially at the executive level. Employers want to see a resume boiled down and well organized.

Nevers

- Never put any emotional information into a resume.
- Never write negative statements about a former employer.
- Never use colored paper.
- Never use your picture or any other personal information like height, weight, or age.
- Don't state information about your religion, color, national origin, or sex.
- Don't include the names of your references on your resume.
- Don't say why you want this job.
- Don't state your objectives. This discussion needs to be left for an interview and wastes valuable resume space. Also, for a resume that undergoes mass mailing, listing an objective can limit your possibilities for other positions in the company.
- Never hedge the truth.
- Never tell anything that happened that was negative.
- Never use abbreviations in place of the word in the job description or accomplishment areas. *Example: Don't say,* Trained in the Clothes dept. before transfer to Seattle store.
- Never use uncommon acronyms without giving the meaning of their letters. The majority of the population knows what CD-ROM is even if they don't know that it is an acronym for Compact Disc-Read-Only Memory. In your work field, if you use acronyms, be sure they are recognizable by potential employers and not just well known at your current position. If in doubt, make sure the acronym has an explanation. Sometimes it is necessary to present both. Some people will more readily recognize the acronym and not the entire meaning.
- Never use *&* in place of the word *and* in a sentence.
- Never use inappropriate capitalization for emphasis. Use only appropriate capitalization. If in doubt, consult *The Gregg Reference Manual.*
- Never overload the text with hyphenated words or phrases in parentheses.

That Final Review

- Make sure you have listed a city and state on all of the company lines.
- Check the font size for faxability.
- Make sure you don't have spacing errors by viewing under Print Preview or by analyzing the printed page.
- Make sure numbers are consistently formatted.
- Make sure work dates are accurate.
- Make sure like items have the same style. For example, all job titles should be preceded by an asterisk and a space and use the same kind of font.
- Current job is in present tense, all the rest are in past tense.
- Use a variety of words that are active and engaging to start your bulleted sentences.
- Make sure that acronyms are handled correctly and sparingly.
- Make sure there are not a lot of long dashes in the writing or over use of parentheses.
- Verify that all sentences have periods. Make sure none were missed.
- At a glance, see if things are in balance and if the information is easy to quickly read.
- Check for undesired font changes on the resume. You can do everything correctly, but sometimes computers do things when you have not chosen to do them. Check over that final resume in printed form.
- Eliminate bad page breaks.
- Be sure the contents of the first page create a powerful and positive impression.
- Eliminate excess or inaccurate boldface or underlining.
- View the resume on the computer with the paragraph marks showing. If you see unequal spacing, it may be due to inconsistent use of paragraph marks other than the Normal style. For example a paragraph mark that is tagged for Company will introduce extra space compared to a paragraph mark tagged for Normal. This can skew the spacing on parts of the resume.

Finally

Put the resume aside for a week, if possible. Rereading it then will allow you to have a fresh view of the content.

When you create the final print, use a good quality white or near-white paper that is twenty-four pound.

Good luck in finding that ideal job.

Surviving the 15-Second Resume Read

Index

statements, useless, 92
style
  creating, 65
  fonts for, 67-68
  issues, 88
  rules, 202, 209-211

T

tags
  creating, 69
  formatting command for styles, 74-75
  naming, 74
  removing space after, 191
  setting, 70
  setting the paragraph, 71
  setting the tab, 72
  for style sheet, 65
  using, 73
tense, 207
Times New Roman, 60
titles, 27
Tool bar, 62
training, special, 50-52
Traynor, Jim, 6-7

U

underlining, 206

V

verbs, action, 196

W

white space, usage, 109, 112
word processor spacing, 208
words
  eliminating redundant, 194
  eliminating vague, 195
work
  description, 38
  experience editing, 92
  experience presentation, 92
  researching position, 38
  titles, 28
work history. *See also* bullets; employment; job;
    professional experience
  agreement with overview, 56
  believability, 39
  check list, 39
  filling out techniques, 150
  format, 46
  guidelines, 44-45
  information critique, 47-48

job titles, 36-37
only one company, 48
quantity, 46
repetition, 46
shaping, 38
using paragraphs, 42
writing better, 197
writing actively, 199

Surviving the 15-Second Resume Read

Yes I want _____ copies of ***Surviving the 15-Second Resume Read*** for $19.95 each plus $3.95 shipping and handling for the first book, 1.95 for additional books. Orders in Colorado, please include applicable sales tax. Canadian orders must include payment in US funds.

Payment must accompany orders. Allow three weeks for delivery. Make checks payable to Hi-Caliber Books.

Orders by Mail
Hi-Caliber Books, LLC
P.O. Box 807
Monument, CO 80132

Order Form

Name	
Organization	
Mailing Address	
City/State/Zip Code	
Phone	
Email	

www.hi-caliberbooks.com
Phone or Fax 719-481-0056